AN INTRODUCTION
TO LAW AND ECONOMICS

AN INTRODUCTION TO LAW AND ECONOMICS

Third Edition

A. MITCHELL POLINSKY

Josephine Scott Crocker Professor
of Law and Economics
Stanford University

76 Ninth Avenue, New York, NY 10011
www.aspenpublishers.com

Permissions
Aspen Publishers
76 Ninth Avenue
New York, NY 10011

Printed in the United States of America

3 4 5 6 7 8 9 0

ISBN 0-7355-3473-X

Library of Congress Cataloging-in-Publication Data

Polinsky, A. Mitchell.
    An introduction to law and economics / A. Mitchell
Polinsky—3rd ed.
        p. cm.
    Includes index.
    ISBN 0-7355-3473-X (alk. paper)
    1. Law and economics.   I. Title.

K487.E3P65 2003
349.73—dc21

                                                            2003048117

About Aspen Publishers

Aspen Publishers, headquartered in New York City, is a leading information provider for attorneys, business professionals, and law students. Written by preeminent authorities, our products consist of analytical and practical information covering both U.S. and international topics. We publish in the full range of formats, including updated manuals, books, periodicals, CDs, and online products.

Our proprietary content is complemented by 2,500 legal databases, containing over 11 million documents, available through our Loislaw division. Aspen Publishers also offers a wide range of topical legal and business databases linked to Loislaw's primary material. Our mission is to provide accurate, timely, and authoritative content in easily accessible formats, supported by unmatched customer care.

To order any Aspen Publishers title, go to *www.aspenpublishers.com* or call 1-800-638-8437.

To reinstate your manual update service, call 1-800-638-8437.

For more information on Loislaw products, go to *www.loislaw.com* or call 1-800-364-2512.

For Customer Care issues, email *CustomerCare@aspenpublishers.com*; call 1-800-234-1660; or fax 1-800-901-9075.

Aspen Publishers
A Wolters Kluwer Company

For

Guido Calabresi and Richard A. Musgrave

*who introduced me
to law and economics*

CONTENTS

LIST OF TABLES

PREFACE

This book studies a limited number of topics in the economic analysis of law in order to focus on "how to think like an economist" about legal rules. As economists know, thinking about a problem like an economist means building a "model" of it — either verbally, graphically, or mathematically — to distill the essence of the relationships being studied. Unfortunately for most law students and many undergraduates, much of the writing by economists about the legal system uses models that are graphical and/or mathematical. The goal of this book is to convey the spirit of the economic approach and the insights gained thereby without the technical apparatus. I will rely solely on simple numerical examples.

Because the book does not presume any knowledge of the legal system, it can be used both in law school and in undergraduate courses on law and economics. In either case, it can supplement a more comprehensive treatment of the subject or be used as the core text with additional material chosen by the instructor. Also, given the topics covered in the book, it can be used to supplement traditional casebooks in first-year law courses on property, contracts, torts, and criminal law, or casebooks in upper-level courses on environmental law.

To make the text flow as smoothly as possible, I have severely limited the number of footnotes. As a general rule, the only footnotes included are those that contain important qualifications or elaborations of points made in the text or that refer the reader to earlier or later discussions in the text. There are three minor exceptions to this rule. First, because I have tried to dispense with the technical terminology of economics as much as possible in the text, I have included some footnotes that relate ideas in the text to this terminology. Second, a few footnotes have been included that cite legal cases or doctrines relevant to points made in the text. And third, whenever the work of a specific author has been referred to in the text, the appropriate citation is included in a footnote. (However, the footnotes do not include any other references to the relevant scholarly literature on the economic analysis of law. Instead, a guide to the literature on which this book is based is provided in a bibliographical appendix.)

In revising the book for the third edition, I have retained the organization and style of the earlier editions. The major substantive change in the present edition is the inclusion of two new chapters. The first analyzes the use of imprisonment as a sanction to deter undesirable conduct, analogous to the treatment of fines in the earlier editions. The other new chapter, on principal-agent liability, addresses whether liability for harm should be imposed on principals (for example, firms) or their agents (such as employees). This question is of broad applicability in the legal system. I also have simplified the bibliographical appendix by omitting reference to many of the early books and journal symposia listed in the first and second editions. This was done both because of the dramatic growth in the literature on law and economics since the second edition — which would have made the bibliographical appendix inordinately long if its earlier style had been maintained — and because several comprehensive bibliographical guides to the literature have appeared since the second edition (to which I provide citations).

I received many helpful comments from colleagues and friends on drafts of the book in its various editions. For their efforts, I wish to thank Lucian Bebchuk, Mark Cohen, Jules Coleman, Robert Cooter, Richard Craswell, John Donohue, Robert Ellickson, Dorsey Ellis, Jr., Nuno Garoupa, Ronald Gilson, Henry Hansmann, Thomas Jackson, Louis Kaplow, Mark Kelman, Alvin Klevorick, Lewis Kornhauser, Steven McBride, Joao de Mello, Peter Menell, Robert Mnookin, Richard Musgrave, Glen Nager, Jeffrey Perloff, Ivan P'ng, Robert Rabin, William Rogerson, Roberta Romano, Daniel Rubinfeld, Steven

Shavell, Gregory Sidak, and Michelle White. Their suggestions substantially improved the final product. I am also grateful to my wife, Joan Roberts Polinsky, for her valuable editorial suggestions; to Barbara Adams for her help in preparing the manuscript of the first edition for publication; and to Morris Ratner for his assistance in updating the bibliography for the second edition.

One final methodological note is in order before proceeding. Economic analysis has been used both to try to explain the legal system as it is and to recommend changes that might improve it. Economists refer to these two approaches respectively as *positive* (or descriptive) economics and *normative* (or prescriptive) economics. As the reader will see, this book is normatively oriented. For each legal application considered, we will determine what legal rule or policy would best promote certain goals — with the primary focus on the goal of efficiency. Because the present legal system undoubtedly has been influenced by efficiency considerations, existing legal rules and policies frequently correspond to those that are optimal in terms of efficiency. To this extent, the book also provides an economic explanation of certain features of the present legal system.

AN INTRODUCTION
TO LAW AND ECONOMICS

CHAPTER 1

INTRODUCTION

When noneconomists want to make fun of economists (or when economists want to make fun of each other), they often tell the following story:

A shipwreck has left a physicist, a chemist, and an economist without food on a deserted island. A few days later a can of beans washes up on the shore. The physicist proposes the following method of opening the can:

> I've calculated that the terminal velocity of a one-pound object — the weight of the can — thrown to a height of twenty feet is 183 feet per second. If we place a rock under the can the impact should just burst the seams without spilling the beans.

The chemist's response is:

> That's risky since we can't be sure we will throw it to the correct height. I've got a better idea. Let's start a fire and heat the can on the coals for one minute, thirty-seven seconds. I've calculated that this should just burst the seams. This method is less risky since we can always push the can off the fire if it starts to burst sooner.

The economist's reaction is:

> Both of your methods may work, but they are too complicated. My approach is much simpler: Assume a can opener.

If you have studied economics before, you will appreciate the significance of this joke (and probably already have heard it more than once). If you have not studied economics, you will soon learn why you should have laughed harder than you did. The can opener story illustrates one important truth and one important lie about economists. The truth is that they approach problems by making assumptions. The lie is that they make ridiculous assumptions (though, unfortunately, this is not always a lie).

The Role of Assumptions

Economists make assumptions for the obvious reason that the world, viewed economically, is too complicated to understand without some abstraction. To see this point in a legal context, consider for example the well-known products liability case of *Escola v. Coca Cola Bottling Co.*, in which the plaintiff was injured by an exploding bottle of soda. In a concurring opinion, Justice Traynor of the California Supreme Court made the following remarks:[1]

> I concur in the judgment [for the plaintiff], but I believe the manufacturer's negligence should no longer be singled out as the basis of a plaintiff's right to recover in cases like the present one. In my opinion it should now be recognized that a manufacturer incurs an absolute liability when an article that he has placed on the market, knowing that it is to be used without inspection, proves to have a defect that causes injury to human beings. . . . Even if there is no negligence, . . . public policy demands that responsibility be fixed wherever it will most effectively reduce the hazards to life and health inherent in defective products that reach the market. It is evident that the manufacturer can anticipate some hazards and guard against the recurrence of others, as the public cannot. Those who suffer injury from defective products are unprepared to meet its consequences. The cost of an injury and the loss of time or health may be an overwhelming misfortune to the person injured, and a needless one, for the risk of injury can be insured by the

1. Escola v. Coca Cola Bottling Co., 24 Cal. 2d 453, 461-462, 150 P.2d 436, 440-441 (1944).

manufacturer and distributed among the public as a cost of doing business. It is to the public interest to discourage the marketing of products having defects that are a menace to the public. If such products nevertheless find their way into the market it is to the public interest to place the responsibility for whatever injury they may cause upon the manufacturer, who, even if he is not negligent in the manufacture of the product, is responsible for its reaching the market. However intermittently such injuries may occur and however haphazardly they may strike, the risk of their occurrence is a constant risk and a general one. Against such a risk there should be general and constant protection and the manufacturer is best situated to afford such protection.

This excerpt from Justice Traynor's opinion implicitly raises several complicated questions but does not go very far in answering them. How is the criterion of "public policy" or "the public interest" to be defined? Should it take into account considerations of both efficiency and equity? What are the effects of the rules of negligence and absolute (or strict) liability on the care exercised by manufacturers in designing and producing products? On the care exercised by consumers in using products? On the price and output of the industry? Do the answers to these questions depend on whether the consumer misperceives the product risks? On whether the victim is a third party rather than a consumer of the product? Should the manufacturer be allowed to raise as a defense that the victim was contributorily negligent in the use of the product? Who is the better bearer of the product risks that are not eliminated — the manufacturer or the consumer? How does the answer to this question depend on whether the manufacturer can self-insure or purchase liability insurance? On whether the consumer can purchase first-party accident insurance or is covered by general social insurance programs?

Unless you are already familiar with the economics literature on products liability, you probably cannot answer many of these questions in a systematic way. By the end of this book, however, you should be able to answer all of them by thinking about them like an economist.

The way an economist would go about answering these

questions would be to isolate one or two of them at a time by making simplifying assumptions that eliminate the others. For example, one might start with the case in which the victim is a consumer of the product and assume that he has perfect information about the product risks, that he does not affect the probability or magnitude of the harm by his own actions, and that he is "risk neutral."[2] It is relatively straightforward in this framework to determine what effects the rules of negligence and strict liability will have on the care exercised by manufacturers and on the price and output of the industry. One then could investigate the consequences of adding the following complications to this framework: consumer misperceptions, joint determination by the manufacturer and the consumer of the probability and magnitude of harm, and "risk aversion" of the consumer (and possibly of the manufacturer).[3] The last complication, risk aversion, would have to be considered both when insurance was and was not assumed to be available.

Each of the special cases just described — corresponding to a particular set of assumptions — can be analyzed relatively easily because only a few issues are considered at a time. Even though each special case is admittedly unrealistic by itself, it will generate some insights that are relevant to real product liability problems. And by examining all of the cases, one can obtain a comprehensive — and, more importantly, comprehensible — perspective on the economics of product liability rules.

This discussion of the role of simplifying assumptions in the economic analysis of product liability rules applies to every problem addressed by economists — including every topic considered in this book. The art of economics is picking assumptions that simplify a problem enough to better understand certain features of it, without causing those features to be unimportant ones. That economists are sometimes (often?) thought to eliminate what is interesting about a problem

---

2. The term "risk neutral" is defined at pp. 30-31 below.
3. The concept of risk aversion is explained at p. 57 below.

through their assumptions is what gives the can opener story its bite.

What has been said thus far is meant to be a warning, not an apology. Be prepared to accept (at least for a while) some obviously unrealistic assumptions. By the end of this book, I hope to convince you that there are many insights to be gained from the economic analysis of law and that these insights are the result of the artful choice of simplifying assumptions.

The plan of the book is somewhat unconventional. Chapters introducing basic economic concepts are interwoven with chapters applying those concepts to legal problems. In this manner, the relevant economic ideas are developed systematically for readers not trained in economics, and readers with some training in economics easily can identify and skip the material with which they are familiar. The economic concepts that are discussed include efficiency and equity, risk bearing and insurance, and competitive markets. These concepts are applied to nuisance law, breach of contract, automobile accidents, law enforcement, pollution control, products liability, principal-agent liability, and litigation. Also, in the concluding chapter, some problems with the practical implementation of the economic approach to law are considered.

The subject matter is introduced in stages of increasing complexity, both to simplify the exposition and to better convey the style of economic analysis. For example, breach of contract remedies are first examined in Chapter 5 in a contractual relationship in which the parties are assumed to be risk neutral. This chapter analyzes the effects of the remedies on the parties' breach decisions and on their "reliance" expenditures. Then, in Chapter 7, the concept of risk aversion is introduced (and the function of insurance is discussed). In Chapter 8, breach of contract remedies are reexamined under the more realistic assumption that the parties may be risk averse. That chapter focuses on the effects of the remedies on the allocation of risk from breaches that do occur. By developing the analysis in these stages, it is easier to see the separate economic functions of breach of contract remedies — to control the behavior of contracting parties with respect to breach and reliance decisions, and to allocate the risks of breaches that do occur. The same pattern is repeated for the discussion of automobile accidents, while the development of each of the other topics — nuisance law, pollution control, law enforcement, products liability, principal-agent liability, and litigation — is contained within a single chapter.

CHAPTER 2

EFFICIENCY AND EQUITY

For purposes of this book, the term *efficiency* will refer to the relationship between the aggregate benefits of a situation and the aggregate costs of the situation;[4] the term *equity* will refer to the distribution of income among individuals.[5] In other words, efficiency corresponds to "the size of the pie," while equity has to do with how it is sliced. Economists traditionally concentrate on how to maximize the size of the pie, leaving to others — such as legislators — the decision how to divide it. The attractiveness of efficiency as a goal is that, under some circumstances described below, everyone can be made better off if society is organized in an efficient manner.

Is There a Conflict?

An important question is whether there is a conflict between the pursuit of efficiency and the pursuit of equity. If

4. This popular concept of efficiency is more intuitive than the technical concept of efficiency known as *Pareto efficiency* or *Pareto optimality* (after the Italian economist Vilfredo Pareto). A situation is said to be Pareto efficient or Pareto optimal if there is no change from that situation that can make someone better off without making someone else worse off. Equivalently, if a situation is *not* efficient in this sense, then, by definition, someone *can* be made better off without making anyone else worse off. Every conclusion in this book regarding the efficiency of a legal rule or policy can be derived in terms of Pareto efficiency or Pareto optimality. I have opted for the more intuitive concept of efficiency used in the text for expositional simplicity.

5. This is the standard sense in which economists use the term *equity*. However, lawyers and philosophers often use this term differently. For example, *equity* might refer to the process by which income or wealth is acquired (as opposed to its final distribution), or to the degree to which exogenously determined rights are protected.

the pie can be sliced in any way desired, then clearly there is no conflict — with a bigger pie, everyone can get a bigger piece. If, however, in order to create a bigger pie, its division must be quite unequal, then, depending on what constitutes an equitable division of the pie, there may well be a conflict between efficiency and equity. It may be preferable to accept a smaller pie (less efficiency) in return for a fairer division (more equity).

The potential conflict between efficiency and equity can be illustrated by a fanciful example. Suppose that the government must decide whether to build a dam and that the Dean of Stanford Law School and I are the only two individuals affected by it. Currently, without the dam, the Dean has $65 and I have $35, so total income is $100. The dam would cost $30 to build, consisting of $30 worth of my labor but none of the Dean's. The dam would create benefits worth $40, all of which would go to the Dean because the only feasible location for building the dam happens to be on her property. Should the dam be built?

On efficiency grounds, the dam clearly should be built because it creates benefits of $40 and costs only $30, thereby creating net benefits of $10. But the equity effects need to be considered as well. Before the dam is built, the Dean has $65 and I have $35. After the dam is built, the Dean will have $105 (including the $40 benefit) and I will have $5 (after subtracting my $30 cost). Whether these distributional consequences are desirable depends on what constitutes a fair distribution of income. Suppose that the most equitable distribution of income involves the Dean receiving 60 percent of total income and my receiving 40 percent. If the dam is not built, then the Dean should have $60 and I should have $40. If the dam is built and total income rises by $10, the Dean should have $66 and I should have $44.

But suppose, regardless of whether the dam is built, it is impossible to redistribute income between the two of us. Therefore, the choice is between the Dean's having $65 and my having $35 if the dam is not built, and the Dean's having $105 and my having $5 if the dam is built. Building the dam is more efficient but less equitable. How this conflict between efficiency and equity should be resolved depends on how important efficiency is relative to equity. If promoting equity is very important, it might be desirable to sacrifice some efficiency for more equity by not building the dam (in other words, "damn" the Dean).

Alternatively, suppose it is possible to costlessly redistribute income between the Dean and me. Then, given the preferred distribution of income, if the dam is not built, $5 would be transferred from the Dean to me, so that she would end up with $60 and I would have $40. If the dam is built, $39 would be transferred to me, so that she would have $66 and I would have $44. Clearly, since total income is distributed according to the percentages desired and we both are better off with the dam, the dam should be built. There is no conflict between efficiency and equity.

Note that, if it is possible to redistribute income at no cost, the dam should be built regardless of what constitutes an equitable distribution of income. If, for example, an egalitarian income distribution is desired, then without the dam the Dean and I each could have $50 and with the dam we each could have $55. If, alternatively, equity required that everything should go to the Dean, the dam should be built because she then could have $110 rather than $100.

The dam example illustrates two important general observations. If income cannot be costlessly redistributed, there may be a conflict between efficiency and equity. Whether there is in fact a conflict depends on the specific distributional consequences of pursuing efficiency and on what constitutes an equitable distribution of income. However, if income can be costlessly redistributed, there is no conflict between efficiency and equity. This is true regardless of the specific distributional consequences of pursuing efficiency and regardless of what constitutes an equitable distribution of income. In other words, if income can be costlessly redistributed, it is always preferable to maximize the size of the pie because the pie can be sliced in any way desired.

Whether income can be costlessly redistributed is discussed in Chapter 17. Although the conclusion there is that income redistribution generally is costly, it is argued nonetheless that efficiency should be the principal criterion for evaluating the legal system. This argument rests on the observations, explained at length in Chapter 17, that it is often impossible to redistribute income through the choice of legal rules and that, even when it is possible, redistribution through the government's tax and transfer system may be cheaper and is likely to be more precise. In other words, the potential conflict between efficiency and equity when income redistribution is costly should be considered in the design of the government's tax and transfer system, but not generally in the choice of legal rules. Thus, *for purposes of discussing the legal system*, a reasonable simplifying assumption is that income can be costlessly redistributed. This assumption will be maintained until Chapter 17 (although the distributional consequences of legal rules occasionally will be noted).

Before proceeding, it is worth mentioning several other standard assumptions of economic analysis that will be made in analyzing the efficiency of legal rules. First, all benefits and costs can be measured in terms of a common denominator — dollars. It is important to emphasize that this assumption is made for expositional simplicity. It is not essential to economic analysis and does not exclude considerations that might be thought of as noneconomic — such as the protection of life and limb.[6] Second, individuals themselves determine the dollar values to place on their benefits and costs. This is known as the assumption of *consumer sovereignty*. It is an acceptable assumption if one believes that individuals generally know what is best for themselves. Third, the values that individuals place on their benefits and costs are "stable" in the sense that these values are not affected by changes in public policy. For example, an individual's evaluation of the desirability of cleaner air is assumed not to depend on whether the legal

---

6. However, to incorporate benefits and costs that are not equivalent to a gain or loss of money would require the introduction of economic concepts that are beyond the scope of this book.

system establishes a right to clean air. This is known as the assumption of *exogenous preferences*. Finally, individuals (and, when relevant, firms) maximize their benefits less their costs. This is known as the assumption of *utility maximization* (or, when firms are involved, profit maximization).

CHAPTER 3

THE COASE THEOREM

One of the central ideas in the economic analysis of law was developed in an article by Ronald H. Coase in 1960.[7] This idea, which has since been named the *Coase Theorem*, is most easily described by an example. Consider a factory whose smoke causes damage to the laundry hung outdoors by five nearby residents. In the absence of any corrective action each resident would suffer $75 in damages, a total of $375. The smoke damage can be eliminated in either of two ways: A smokescreen can be installed on the factory's chimney, at a cost of $150, or each resident can be provided an electric dryer, at a cost of $50 per resident. The efficient solution is clearly to install the smokescreen because it eliminates total damages of $375 for an outlay of only $150, and it is cheaper than purchasing five dryers for $250.

Zero Transaction Costs

The question asked by Coase was whether the efficient outcome would result if the right to clean air is assigned to the residents or if the right to pollute is given to the factory. If there is a right to clean air, then the factory has three choices: pollute and pay $375 in damages, install a smokescreen for $150, or purchase five dryers for the residents at a total cost of $250. Clearly, the factory would install the smokescreen, the efficient solution. If there is a right to pollute, then the

7. Ronald H. Coase, The Problem of Social Cost, 3 J.L. & Econ. 1 (1960).

residents face three choices: suffer their collective damages of $375, purchase five dryers for $250, or buy a smokescreen for the factory for $150. The residents also would purchase the smokescreen. In other words, the efficient outcome will be achieved regardless of the assignment of the legal right.

It was implicitly assumed in this example that the residents could costlessly get together and negotiate with the factory. In Coase's language, this is referred to as the assumption of *zero transaction costs.* In general, transaction costs include the costs of identifying the parties with whom one has to bargain, the costs of getting together with them, the costs of the bargaining process itself, and the costs of enforcing any bargain reached. With this general definition of transaction costs in mind, we can now state the simple version of the Coase Theorem: If there are zero transaction costs, the efficient outcome will occur regardless of the choice of legal rule.

Note that, although the choice of the legal rule does not affect the attainment of the efficient solution when there are zero transaction costs, it does affect the distribution of income. If the residents have the right to clean air, the factory pays $150 for the smokescreen, whereas if the factory has the right to pollute, the residents pay for the smokescreen. Thus, the choice of the legal rule redistributes income by the amount of the least-cost solution to the conflict. Because it is assumed for now that income can be costlessly redistributed, this distributional effect is of no consequence — if it is not desired, it can be easily corrected.

Positive Transaction Costs

The assumption of zero transaction costs obviously is unrealistic in many conflict situations. At the very least, the disputing parties usually would have to spend time and/or money to get together to discuss the dispute. To see the consequences of positive transaction costs, suppose in the example that it costs each resident $60 to get together with the others (due, say, to transportation costs and the value attached to time). If the residents have a right to clean air, the factory again faces the choice of paying damages, buying a smokescreen, or buying five dryers. The factory again would purchase the smokescreen, the efficient solution. If the factory has a right to pollute, each resident now has to decide whether to bear the losses of $75, buy a dryer for $50, or get together with the other residents for $60 to collectively buy a smokescreen for $150. Clearly, each resident will choose to purchase a dryer, an inefficient outcome. Thus, given the transaction costs described, the right to clean air is efficient, but the right to pollute is not.

Note that in the example the preferred legal rule minimized the effects of transaction costs in the following sense. Under the right to clean air, the factory had to decide whether to pay damages, install a smokescreen, or buy five dryers. Because it was not necessary for the factory to get together with the residents to decide what to do, the transaction costs — the costs of the residents to get together — did not have any effect. Under the right to pollute, the residents had to decide what to do. Because the residents were induced to choose an inefficient solution in order to avoid the cost of getting together, the transaction costs did have an effect. Thus, even though no transaction costs were actually incurred under the right to pollute because the residents did not get together, the effects of transaction costs were greater under that rule.

We can now state the more complicated version of the Coase Theorem: If there are positive transaction costs, the efficient outcome may not occur under every legal rule. In these circumstances, the preferred legal rule is the rule that minimizes the effects of transaction costs. These effects include actually incurring transaction costs as well as the inefficient choices induced by a desire to avoid transaction costs.

The distributional consequences of legal rules are somewhat more complicated when there are transaction costs. It is no longer true, as it was when there were zero transaction costs, that the choice of the rule redistributes income by the amount of the least-cost solution. In the example, if the residents have the right to clean air, the factory pays $150 for the smokescreen, whereas if the factory has the right to pollute, the residents pay $250 for five dryers.

Although the simple version of the Coase Theorem makes an unrealistic assumption about transaction costs, it provides a useful way to begin thinking about legal problems because it suggests the kinds of transactions that would have to occur under each legal rule in order for that rule to be efficient. Once these required transactions are identified, it may be apparent that, given more realistic assumptions about transaction costs, one rule clearly is preferable to another on efficiency grounds. The more complicated version of the Coase Theorem provides a guide to choosing legal rules in this situation. All of the applications investigated in this book — nuisance law, breach of contract, automobile accidents, law enforcement, pollution control, products liability, principal-agent liability, and litigation — can be approached in this way, although some fit more naturally into the Coasian framework than others.

CHAPTER 4

FIRST APPLICATION — NUISANCE LAW

One area of law that can be readily examined in terms of the Coase Theorem is nuisance law. Nuisance cases result from incompatible land uses and typically involve a small number of individuals bargaining with each other, as when emissions from a factory fall upon neighboring property, bright lights or noise disturb someone's sleep, or an unsightly building spoils an attractive residential neighborhood.

Adopting a framework first suggested by Guido Calabresi and A. Douglas Melamed,[8] the resolution of a nuisance dispute may be viewed as involving two steps. First, an *entitlement* must be chosen — that is, a determination must be made regarding who is entitled to prevail. The injurer can be granted the right to engage in the activity that causes harm, or the victim can be granted the right to be free from harm. Then, a decision must be made about how to protect the entitlement. One possibility is to grant the holder of the entitlement an *injunction*. If the victim holds the entitlement, protecting it by an injunction means that he can prohibit the injurer from causing harm. Thus, the injurer can cause damage only if he "buys off" the victim. Similarly, if the injurer holds the entitlement, protecting it by an injunction means that the victim must buy off the injurer if he wants damages reduced.

An alternative method of protecting entitlements is to

8. Guido Calabresi & A. Douglas Melamed, Property Rules, Liability Rules and Inalienability: One View of the Cathedral, 85 Harv. L. Rev. 1089 (1972).

TABLE 1

Nuisance Law Example

Output of Factory	Additional Profits of Factory	Total Profits of Factory	Additional Damages of Resident	Total Damages of Resident	Total Profits Less Total Damages
0	—	$0	—	$0	$0
1	$10,000	$10,000	$1,000	$1,000	$9,000
2	$4,000	$14,000	$15,000	$16,000	−$2,000
3	$2,000	$16,000	$20,000	$36,000	−$20,000

give the holder of the entitlement an amount of money — *damages* — that some governmental body, such as a court, determines. If the victim has the entitlement, he has the right to be compensated, but he cannot prohibit the injurer from causing harm as he could under an injunctive remedy.[9] Analogously, if the injurer holds the entitlement, protecting it by a damage remedy would mean that the victim could restrict the injurer's activity but would have to compensate the injurer for the injurer's "damages" (for example, forgone profits). This last combination — entitling the injurer to damages — is very unconventional, but it has been used.[10] Thus, there are four possible solutions, corresponding to who is given the entitlement and how it is protected.

In this chapter, we will examine whether the efficiency criterion can determine which entitlement to choose and which remedy to use to protect it. The analysis will be based on an example of a polluting factory located next to a single resident. The facts of the example are described in Table 1. The factory can produce zero, one, two, or three units of output. Increasing output results in additional profits for the factory and additional damages to the resident. If the factory produces

9. A leading American nuisance case illustrating this version of the damage remedy is Boomer v. Atlantic Cement Co., 26 N.Y.2d 219, 257 N.E.2d 870, 309 N.Y.S.2d 312 (1970).

10. See Spur Industries, Inc. v. Del E. Webb Development Co., 108 Ariz. 178, 494 P.2d 700 (1972).

one unit, the factory obtains $10,000 in profits and the resident suffers $1,000 in damages. Total profits less total damages are $9,000. If the factory produces a second unit, the factory's additional profits are $4,000 — so the factory's total profits are $14,000 — and the resident's additional damages are $15,000 — so the resident's total damages are $16,000. Then total profits less total damages are −$2,000. If the factory produces a third unit, the results are described similarly.

Maximizing the size of the pie in the nuisance law example is equivalent to maximizing the factory's profits net of the resident's damages. Given the data in Table 1, this occurs when the factory produces one unit of output (see the last column). Thus, one unit of output is the efficient solution.

Zero Transaction Costs

We know from the discussion in the previous chapter that if there are zero transaction costs, then the factory will end up producing the efficient output regardless of the choice of remedy or entitlement. It will be useful to see how this comes about in the example before considering more realistic assumptions about transaction costs.

Under the injunctive remedy, suppose, for example, that an entitlement to clean air is given to the resident. This corresponds to giving the resident the right to force the factory to produce zero output. The factory, however, would gain $10,000 in profits from producing one unit, and the resident would suffer only $1,000 in damages. Thus, it is in each party's interest to reach an agreement in which the factory would pay the resident some amount between $1,000 and $10,000 for permission to produce one unit. Assuming zero transaction costs, which is interpreted to imply cooperative behavior, such an agreement will be reached. It will not be mutually beneficial for the factory to produce a second unit because the factory would gain only an additional $4,000, whereas the resident would suffer an additional $15,000 in damages. Similarly, it would not be mutually beneficial for the factory to produce three units. Thus, the parties would remain at one unit, the efficient solution.

Under the damage remedy, suppose that an entitlement to clean air is given to the resident, as before, and that the court makes the factory liable for the resident's actual damages. Because the factory would gain $10,000 from producing one unit and would be liable for only $1,000, the factory clearly will choose to produce at least one unit. It will not be in the factory's interest to produce the second unit because the increase in the factory's profits is $4,000 and its additional liability is $15,000. Similarly, the factory would be worse off if it produced three units. Thus, the factory would choose to produce the efficient output.

Strategic Behavior

The assumption of zero transaction costs obviously is unrealistic in many respects. We will first consider the possibility that the parties will behave strategically;[11] for instance, to establish reputations as tough bargainers, they may "hold out" for a disproportionate share of the gains from any agreement. If both parties are stubborn, they may not be able to reach an agreement even when both could be made better off. Such behavior is not uncommon; for example, parties often go to court rather than settle out of court more cheaply.[12] We will now reconsider the nuisance remedies assuming that the parties behave strategically.

Under the injunctive remedy with an entitlement to clean air, we saw that it would be in each party's interest to reach an agreement in which the factory paid the resident some

11. Although strategic behavior does not necessarily generate any out-of-pocket costs or costs associated with lost time, it will be treated as a type of transaction cost. It is like other transaction costs in that it may prevent the parties from reaching an efficient agreement.

12. There may be reasons other than strategic behavior why parties litigate rather than settle. For example, the parties may disagree about the plaintiff's chance of winning at trial and therefore may not perceive a mutually beneficial settlement. See Chapter 16 below.

amount between $1,000 and $10,000. However, because of strategic behavior, the resident may, for example, hold out for $8,000, while the factory may refuse to pay anything over $5,000. As a result, the resident might enforce the injunction and shut down the factory (at least for some period), an inefficient outcome.

The problem of strategic behavior under the injunctive remedy can be overcome by the appropriate choice of the entitlement. Instead of an entitlement corresponding to zero output of the factory — an *absolute* entitlement to clean air — suppose that the court were to choose an entitlement corresponding to one unit of output — an *intermediate* entitlement. Under the injunctive remedy, this would mean that the factory could produce one unit, but no more, without having to obtain the permission of the resident. Starting at one unit of output, it would not be mutually beneficial to produce a second or third unit because the factory's gains are less than the resident's losses. Likewise, it would not be mutually beneficial to reduce output to zero because the resident's gain (in the form of reduced damages) is less than the factory's loss (in the form of reduced profits). Thus, starting at an intermediate entitlement of one unit, the parties will remain there. Strategic behavior cannot upset this outcome because no beneficial changes can be made that would require negotiation.

This discussion illustrates a general principle: Under the injunctive remedy, to overcome strategic behavior it is necessary to choose an entitlement corresponding to the efficient outcome. This is because, starting from any other entitlement, the parties must reach an agreement to get to the efficient outcome; and strategic behavior may prevent this agreement from being reached.

Under the damage remedy with an entitlement to clean air and liability equal to actual damages, we saw that the factory would choose to produce the efficient output of one unit. The presence of strategic behavior does not affect this result because there are no bargains that the parties have to reach. Also, there are no threats the factory can make because, given that the factory is liable for actual damages, the resident is indifferent among all levels of the factory's output.

It is essential to the conclusion of the previous paragraph that liability equals actual damages. To see why, suppose that the factory's liability is $7,000 for the first unit — exceeding the resident's damages of $1,000 — and, as before, is equal to the resident's damages for the second and third units. If the factory produces one unit of output it will gain $3,000 ($10,000 − $7,000). The resident also will gain $6,000, the amount by which the liability payment exceeds actual damages ($7,000 − $1,000). But the factory can deny this gain to the resident by not producing the first unit of output. Therefore, if the factory believes that it can bargain more effectively than the resident, it may threaten to not produce unless the resident pays some specified amount up to his full gain of $6,000. However, if the resident believes that he is the better bargainer, he may not give in to the factory's demand. As a result, the factory may carry out its threat, if only to make future threats credible, and produce at an inefficient output.

The kind of "extortion" threat just described cannot occur if liability is equal to actual damages. Because the resident then is not overcompensated, and so gains nothing from an increase in the factory's output, the factory's threat to not produce the first unit of output has no effect. With full compensation, the resident is indifferent to whether the first unit is produced and is likewise indifferent with respect to the second and third units. Thus, the factory will maximize its after-liability profits by increasing production to the efficient output of one unit.

This discussion illustrates another general principle: Under the damage remedy, to overcome strategic behavior it is necessary to set liability equal to actual damages. If liability exceeds actual damages, then the party who is liable has an incentive to threaten to deny the other party's overcompensation by choosing an inefficient outcome.[13]

---

13. More generally, strategic behavior can be overcome under the damage remedy if liability is less than or equal to actual damages up to the efficient output and greater than or equal to actual damages beyond the efficient output. It is beyond the scope of this chapter to explain this more general proposition. Note, however, that the statements and examples in the text are consistent with it.

Imperfect Information

The analysis of strategic behavior under the injunctive and damage remedies suggests another way in which the assumption of zero transaction costs is likely to be unrealistic. For both remedies, it was seen that the court must have certain information about the nuisance dispute in order to achieve the efficient solution. Under the injunctive remedy, the court needs to know the efficient outcome to choose an entitlement corresponding to it. And under the damage remedy, the court needs to know the resident's damages to set liability equal to actual damages. It was implicitly assumed that the court had whatever information was required. We will now reconsider the remedies when this information is incomplete. The assumption of strategic behavior will be maintained in this discussion.

Suppose that the court has limited information of the following sort: It knows the resident's schedule of damages but does not know the factory's schedule of profits. For example, the court might easily be able to obtain information about the damage to property from pollution but not about the cost to the polluter of changing production methods to abate pollution.[14]

Under the injunctive remedy, the court no longer can achieve the efficient outcome. To reach that outcome, strategic behavior must be avoided, which requires under the injunctive remedy that the entitlement coincide with the efficient output. But to determine the efficient output, the court must know when the factory's profits net of the resident's damages are maximized. Knowing the damage schedule alone obviously is insufficient to determine this level of output. Although the court could attempt to estimate the efficient output, if it makes a mistake, as it generally will, strategic behavior may prevent the parties from bargaining to the efficient output.

The damage remedy can reach the efficient outcome de-

14. The alternative case in which the court knows the factory's profit schedule but not the resident's damage schedule will not be analyzed because it is analogous to the case discussed in the text.

spite the court's imperfect information. This result can be guaranteed, however, only if the court gives an absolute entitlement to clean air to the resident and sets liability equal to actual damages. Any other entitlement might lead to the efficient outcome, but it need not. For example, suppose that the court assigns an intermediate entitlement to pollute to the factory corresponding to two units of output and makes the factory liable thereafter for the resident's damages. Initially, the factory would choose to produce two units because there is no liability up to and including the second unit, and liability for the third unit — equal to the resident's damages of $20,000 — exceeds the factory's additional profits — equal to $2,000. The resident then would have an incentive to "bribe" the factory to reduce output from two units to the efficient output of one unit, but because of strategic behavior the parties might not reach that output.

On the other hand, if the court chooses an entitlement corresponding to zero or one unit of output and sets liability thereafter equal to actual damages, the damage remedy will lead the factory to produce at the efficient output. In other words, with liability equal to actual damages, the damage remedy leads to the efficient outcome if, and only if, the entitlement is at or below the efficient output. However, because the court cannot determine the efficient output with its limited information, the only way it can guarantee the efficient result is to choose the entitlement corresponding to the lowest possible output — an absolute entitlement to the resident.

The discussion thus far has shown that if the court knows the victim's schedule of damages but not the injurer's schedule of profits, it generally cannot implement an efficient injunctive remedy but it can implement an efficient damage remedy. However, in many nuisance situations the court might not be able to easily determine the victim's damages. For example, although a court might be able to accurately estimate the market price of someone's home, this price generally is less than the damages that would be suffered by the resident if he were forced to move, because it does not reflect the special attachment he might have for that location and house. Damages often include a subjective or idiosyncratic element of this sort that is difficult or impossible to measure.[15] We will therefore briefly reconsider the remedies when the court is assumed to underestimate the resident's damages (and, as before, to not know anything about the factory's profits). For concreteness, suppose in the example that the court's estimate of damages is $500 per unit of output.

Because the court obviously still cannot implement an efficient injunctive remedy, the discussion will focus on the damage remedy. Suppose an absolute entitlement is awarded to the resident. If damages were measured accurately, then, as we saw above, the damage remedy would lead to the efficient outcome. Now, however, with damages underestimated, the factory generally will overshoot the efficient output. In the example, with liability equal to $500 per unit of output, the factory will choose to produce three units because its additional profit from producing each unit exceeds $500 (see Table 1).

Starting at an output of three units, the resident would be better off by $19,500 if output were reduced by one unit — he would lose a $500 liability payment, but his damages would decline by $20,000 (see Table 1). The factory would lose only $1,500 by this change — its profits would fall by $2,000, but it would avoid a $500 liability payment. Thus, if the parties could reach an agreement in which the resident paid the factory some amount between $1,500 and $19,500 to reduce output by one unit, both parties would be better off. However, because of strategic behavior, such a deal will not necessarily occur. And even if an agreement were reached with respect to this unit, the parties might fail to reach an agreement when they negotiate over reducing output from two units to the efficient output of one unit.

The general point of this discussion can be simply stated. If courts underestimate the victim's damages, then the damage remedy initially will lead to an excessive output and this inefficiency may not be corrected because of strategic behavior. There is then no general reason to believe that a damage remedy would be preferable to an injunctive remedy. For example,

15. In practice, this element of damages generally is excluded from a damage award.

suppose that, starting with an absolute entitlement to the resident, the damage remedy would lead to an output of three units for the reasons described in the previous paragraph, and the injunctive remedy would lead to an output of zero units because of strategic behavior. The injunctive outcome then is more efficient than the damage outcome because total profits less total damages are $0 rather than $-\$20,000$ (see Table 1). In general, however, either remedy could be the more efficient one.

We can now summarize the results in this chapter regarding the efficiency analysis of nuisance remedies. If the parties can be expected to bargain cooperatively (and there are no other transaction costs), then every choice of entitlement and remedy will be efficient. If the parties are likely to act strategically, then the efficient outcome still can be achieved under both remedies if the court has adequate information. Strategic behavior can be overcome under the injunctive remedy by choosing the entitlement that corresponds to the efficient outcome, which can be determined only if the court knows the injurer's benefits from engaging in the harmful activity and the victim's damages. And strategic behavior can be overcome under the damage remedy by giving an absolute entitlement to the victim and setting liability equal to actual damages, which obviously requires knowledge of the victim's damages. If the court only knows the victim's damages, the injunctive remedy generally will fail because the court cannot accurately set the entitlement equal to the efficient outcome, but the damage remedy still can guarantee the efficient outcome. However, if the court underestimates the victim's damages, then the damage remedy generally will lead to excessive output and may be less desirable than the injunctive remedy.

Although in theory either remedy could therefore be more efficient, it may be apparent in particular circumstances that one remedy is likely to be better than the other. For example, suppose that a court is confident that its estimate of the victim's damages is close to the truth, but believes that its estimate of the injurer's benefits is inaccurate. Then an entitlement to the victim protected by a damage remedy generally would be preferred because this would be likely to lead to an outcome close to the efficient solution. Alternatively, suppose that a court has poor information both about the victim's damages and the injurer's benefits, but is confident that the efficiency loss from too little activity by the injurer is small relative to the efficiency loss from excessive activity. Then an entitlement to the victim protected by an injunctive remedy would be desirable because this would guarantee that the final outcome will not be too bad. Thus, the efficiency analysis of nuisance law may be helpful even when there is some uncertainty about which entitlement and remedy to choose.

CHAPTER 5
SECOND APPLICATION —
BREACH OF CONTRACT

Another area of law that can be discussed within the Coasian framework of bargaining among a small number of individuals is contract law. Unlike the normal nuisance law situation, however, the parties to a contract negotiate with each other before any dispute arises. Since the parties can decide in advance how to resolve potential disputes, it might be asked whether it is necessary or desirable to have general legal rules governing contract disputes. The reason contract rules are desirable is, of course, that it would be prohibitively costly (if even possible) to negotiate and draft a contract that provides for every conceivable contingency. For contingencies that are thought to be unlikely or that do not affect the parties' costs and benefits very much, it is not worth going to the trouble to specify in advance what to do if the contingency should occur.

Contract law can be viewed as filling in these "gaps" in the contract — attempting to reproduce what the parties would have agreed to if they could have costlessly planned for the event initially. Since the parties would have included contract terms that maximize their joint benefits net of their joint costs — both parties can thereby be made better off — this approach is equivalent to designing contract law according to the efficiency criterion.[16]

16. The statement that the parties would have maximized their joint benefits net of their joint costs obviously presumes that they would have bargained cooperatively. Also, the conclusion that the maximization of the parties' joint benefits net of their joint costs is the goal of efficiency presumes that no one else is affected by the contract.

In the left margin, handwritten vertically: *B4. outside the remedies*

In this chapter, we will examine three remedies for breach of contract from this perspective. One, *expectation damages*, awards the breached-against party an amount of money that puts him in the same position he would have been in had the contract been completed. Another, *reliance damages*, awards an amount of money that places the breached-against party in the position he would have been in had he never entered into the contract initially. The last, *restitution damages*, awards the breached-against party an amount of money corresponding to any benefits that he has conferred upon the breaching party.[17]

The analysis will be undertaken using an example in which a seller, *S*, can produce a good called a "widget" for $150. Widgets are not generally available. For this reason, a buyer, *B1*, who values the widget at $200, enters into a contract with *S* for the future delivery of a widget. The contract price is paid in advance. In order to use the widget, *B1* must make an expenditure of $10 prior to delivery (for example, he might have to modify his warehouse slightly to store the widget). This will be referred to as his *reliance expenditure* or *reliance investment*. If the contract is not completed, this expenditure is assumed to have no value.[18]

Before delivery occurs, there is a chance that some other buyer, *B2*, may also want the widget. The value *B2* attaches to the widget is not known at the time *S* and *B1* enter into their contract. For simplicity, it is assumed that *B2*'s value will be either $0, $180, or $250, and that he will offer this amount for it. Thus, after *S* and *B1* have entered into their contract, there is a chance that *B2* will offer more for the widget than *B1* did — certainly if *B2*'s value is $250. Both *S* and *B1* are assumed to be aware of these possibilities. The facts of this example are summarized in Table 2 (ignore for now the note at the bottom of the table).

It also will be assumed in this chapter that the parties are

17. Another remedy, liquidated damages, will be discussed in Chapter 8 below.

18. The assumptions that the contract price is paid in advance and that the reliance investment has no value in the event of breach are not essential and do not affect any of the general conclusions in this chapter.

TABLE 2

Breach of Contract Example

S is the seller:

    S's cost to produce the widget is $150.

B1 is the initial buyer:

    B1 values the widget at $200.

    B1's reliance expenditure is $10.[a]

    B1 pays S the contract price in advance.

B2 is the second buyer:

    B2 values the widget at $0 or $180 or $250.

    a. The possibility that B1 can spend an additional $24 on reliance and thereby increase the value of the widget to him by $30 also is considered.

risk neutral. This means that they only care about the *expected value* of a risky situation — that is, the magnitude of a potential loss or gain multiplied by the probability of the loss or gain occurring. For example, the expected gain in a situation involving a 50 percent chance of winning $10,000 is $5,000. A risk-neutral person would, by definition, be indifferent between this situation and any other one with the same expected gain — such as a situation involving a 25 percent chance of winning $20,000, or one involving a certainty of winning $5,000.

A Fully Specified Contract

Before considering how breach of contract remedies fill in the gaps in incompletely specified contracts, it will be useful to examine the contract between S and B1 when everything is specified in advance. Suppose the contract has the following provisions. First, the contract price, payable in advance, is $175. Second, if the value B2 attaches to the widget is $0 or $180, then S is to deliver the widget to B1. In this case, S's profit is $25 — the contract price of $175 less S's production cost of $150 — and B1's profit is $15 — the $200 value to B1 less his $10 reliance expenditure and less the contract price of $175. Third, the contract states that in the event that B2 values the widget at $250, S is to sell it to B2 rather than B1, but then must pay B1 $225. In this case S's profit is $50 — the contract price of $175 less S's production cost of $150 plus B2's payment to S of $250 less S's payment to B1 of $225. B1's profit is then $40 — the $225 payment from S less the reliance expenditure of $10 and less the contract price paid in advance of $175.

It is clear that this fully specified contract between S and B1 is efficient. The only choice the parties have to make that affects their *joint* profits is whether S is to sell to B2 if B2 wants the widget. If S does not sell to B2, then the joint profits of S and B1 are $40 — S's profit of $25 plus B1's profit of $15. If S does sell to B2 when B2 values the widget at $250, then the joint profits of S and B1 rise to $90 — S's profit of $50 plus B1's profit of $40. However, if S were to sell to B2 when B2 values the widget at $180, the joint profits of S and B1 would fall to $20 because, together, they would have revenue of $180 and costs of $160 (S's production cost of $150 plus B1's reliance expenditure of $10). Thus, the provisions in the contract that call for S to sell the widget to B2 if B2 values it at $250 but not if he values it at $0 or $180 are efficient.[19]

It is important to note that there is a close relationship between the contract price and the amount of money S has to pay to B1 if S sells the widget to B2. In general, the higher the amount paid to B1, the higher the contract price. For example, suppose S has to pay B1 $240 rather than $225 in the event that the widget is sold to B2. B1 clearly would prefer to receive the higher payment in the event of a breach, and S clearly would prefer to pay the lower amount. Presumably, therefore,

19. Since B2 is assumed to offer an amount equal to the value he attaches to the widget, his profits are not affected by how valuable the widget is to him. This is why B2's profits do not need to be taken into account in determining the efficient contract provisions.

S will demand, and *B1* will be willing to offer, a higher contract price in advance — say $180 instead of $175.

Efficient Breach

Thus far, the example illustrates a simple but fundamental principle in the economic analysis of contract law: A fully specified contract is efficient. In practice, however, the cost of contracting will lead the parties to ignore relatively unimportant contingencies. Therefore, now suppose that because *S* and *B1* believe that an offer from *B2* is unlikely, they do not bother to include a provision in the contract that deals with the possibility that *B2* will offer more for the widget. The contract simply states that *S* is to deliver a widget to *B1* at some price payable in advance. We will now examine whether the expectation, reliance, and restitution remedies for breach of contract are efficient alternatives to an explicit contract provision regarding when the widget should be sold to *B2* rather than to *B1*. An important assumption in the following analysis is that if *S* wants to breach the contract, *B1* will not find it worthwhile (because of bargaining costs) to attempt to stop *S* from breaching or to repurchase the widget from *B2* after the breach. (If it were costless for *B1* to negotiate with *S* or *B2*, then the Coasian analysis in Chapter 3 implies that every remedy would be efficient.)

First consider a breach of the contract when the expectation remedy is applicable. If the contract had been completed, *B1* would have made a profit equal to the $200 value he places on the widget less his reliance expenditure and less the contract price he paid in advance. Thus, to put *B1* in the same position he would have been in had the contract been completed, it is necessary to compensate *B1* $200 (because *B1* has already incurred the reliance expense and has paid *S* the contract price). Given a damage payment of $200, *S* will decide to breach if *B2* offers $250 for the widget, but not if he offers $180 (or, of course, $0). Thus, the expectation remedy leads to the efficient outcome. Put differently, the expectation remedy is an efficient substitute for explicit contract provisions governing breach. It thereby saves the parties the cost and inconvenience of dealing with unlikely contingencies every time they enter into a contract. Instead, they can simply rely on a breach of contract remedy in the few instances when the issue of breach arises.

Note that the conclusion that the expectation remedy induces efficient breach decisions does not depend on what the actual contract price is. S will have to pay B1 $200 in the event of a breach regardless of the contract price because, given that B1 paid the contract price (and incurred the reliance expense) in advance, $200 is the amount of money necessary to put B1 in the same position he would have been in had the contract been completed. Thus, regardless of the contract price, S will breach in order to sell to B2 only if B2 offers more than $200 for the widget.

Next consider the reliance remedy. If B1 had not entered into the contract with S, it is assumed that he would have earned zero profit.[20] Thus, to put B1 in the same position he would have been in had he never entered into the contract, it is necessary to compensate B1 for his $10 reliance investment and to return to him the contract price that he paid in advance. In other words, the reliance measure of damages equals the reliance expenditure plus the contract price.

To determine the effects of the reliance remedy on S's decision to breach, it is therefore necessary to discuss the setting of the contract price. Since S's production cost is $150, he will not be willing to accept less than this amount. B1 will be willing to pay up to $190 for the widget because he values it at $200 but has to make the $10 reliance investment. Thus, the contract price will be somewhere between $150 and $190, the exact price depending on the relative bargaining strengths of the parties. Suppose, for concreteness, that it is $160.

Given a reliance expenditure of $10 and a contract price of $160, the reliance remedy would award B1 $170 in the event of a breach by S. Therefore, S will breach the contract if B2

20. This assumption is not essential and does not affect any of the general conclusions about the reliance remedy.

offers either $180 or $250 for the widget because S has to pay only $170 in damages. If $B2$'s value is $180, the breach will be inefficient because the value $B2$ attaches to the widget is less than the $200 value $B1$ attaches to it. In other words, the reliance remedy may lead to an inefficient breach.

Finally, consider the restitution remedy. The only benefit $B1$ has conferred on S has been that he paid the contract price in advance. Thus, to award $B1$ an amount of money corresponding to the benefit he has conferred, it is necessary to force S to return the contract price to $B1$. In other words, restitution damages equal the contract price. For the same reasons discussed with respect to the reliance remedy, the contract price will be somewhere between $150 and $190. If it is below $180, then the restitution remedy also will lead to an inefficient breach when $B2$ values the widget at $180.

In general, the restitution remedy is more likely to lead to inefficient breaches than the reliance remedy for the following reasons. First note that the contract price under the restitution remedy generally would be less than the contract price under the reliance remedy. Intuitively, this is because the seller (S in the example) does not have to compensate the buyer ($B1$ in the example) for his reliance expenditure under the restitution remedy, but he does have to under the reliance remedy. Consequently, the buyer presumably would not be willing to pay as much for the contract under the restitution remedy, and the seller presumably would be willing to accept less. Given a lower contract price under the restitution remedy, the damage payment also would be lower under that remedy because restitution damages equal the contract price, whereas reliance damages equal the contract price plus the reliance expenditure. One would expect inefficient breaches to be more likely under the restitution remedy because of the lower damage payment.

The discussion thus far illustrates several general conclusions about the economic effects of contract law. The key result is that the expectation remedy is the only remedy that creates efficient incentives with respect to breaches of contracts. This is because the expectation remedy forces the breaching party to pay in damages the value of the good to the breached-against party. If another buyer values the good more than this, then it is efficient for that buyer to have the good. Given the expectation measure of damages, the seller will have an incentive to breach in order to obtain the higher offer. If another buyer values the good less than the original buyer, a breach is not efficient and the expectation remedy will appropriately discourage breaches. Any other measure of damages for breach of contract generally will be inefficient. If damages exceed expectation damages, then a breach might not occur even though it would be efficient. For example, if damages were $260 in the example, then S would not breach when B2 offers $250. And if damages are below expectation damages, an inefficient breach might occur. This is the problem with the reliance remedy, because it leads to a level of damages below the expectation level. The restitution remedy is even worse because it provides less than the reliance measure of damages.

Efficient Reliance

Inducing optimal breaches of contracts is not the only problem with which contract law has to deal. Another issue of concern relates to reliance expenditures. In the example, it was assumed that B1's reliance investment was fixed at $10. In general, this expenditure can vary, and the more spent on reliance, the more valuable the contract will be to the buyer if it is completed. For example, the buyer might be able to purchase various customized pieces of equipment, each of which is capable of transforming the widget into a more valuable final product. (Because widgets are perishable, this equipment must be obtained before delivery.) In the remainder of this chapter we will analyze how remedies for breach of contract affect the amount invested in reliance.

In order to examine the reliance decision, the example used earlier must be made slightly more complicated. It still will be assumed that the original buyer B1 must spend at least $10 on reliance and that the widget will be worth $200 to him if this is all that he spends. But now he will have the option of spending an *additional* $24 on reliance and thereby raising the value of the widget to him by $30. As before, if the contract is not completed, the reliance expenditure will have no value. It also will be assumed that the three values the second buyer B2 might attach to the widget — $0, $180, or $250 — are all equally likely. The relevance of this assumption will become apparent shortly.

Although it might seem that the efficiency criterion would dictate having B1 make the additional reliance investment — because this investment seems to increase the value of the widget by $30 at a cost of only $24 — this conclusion is incorrect. The increase in value occurs only if the contract is completed and B1 obtains the widget. But, as we have seen, it is efficient for S to breach the contract with B1 in order to sell to B2 if the value of the widget to B2 turns out to be $250. Given the assumption at the end of the previous paragraph, there is a one-in-three chance that B2 will value the widget this much. In other words, if the breach decision is efficient, there is only a two-thirds chance that B1 will obtain the widget. Thus, while the $24 cost of reliance is certain, the $30 benefit from reliance is uncertain. The *expected* benefit — the benefit multiplied by the probability of its realization — is only $20. It is inefficient to incur a $24 cost to obtain a $20 expected benefit.

If S and B1 had been able to costlessly negotiate and draft their contract initially, they would have included a provision that specified that B1 is not to make the additional $24 reliance investment. However, negotiating over B1's reliance decision is not a simple matter. For example, if it is difficult for S to verify how much additional benefit B1 would obtain from the additional reliance expenditure, B1 might be able to take advantage of S's imperfect information. Thus, analogously to the breach of contract decision, it is reasonable to consider the possibility that a provision regarding the reliance decision was not included in the contract. We will therefore examine whether some breach of contract remedy can serve as a substitute for this provision.

Under the expectation remedy, B1 either will receive the widget (if the contract is performed) or be given an amount of money equivalent to the value of the widget (if the contract is breached). If *B1* spends just $10 on reliance, the widget will be worth $200 to him, so expectation damages would equal $200. If he spends an additional $24 on reliance, the widget will be worth an additional $30 to him, so expectation damages would equal $230. Thus, by spending an extra $24, he will obtain a $30 benefit either because the widget will be delivered or higher expectation damages will be paid. Clearly, *B1* will invest the additional $24 in reliance, an inefficient outcome for the reasons discussed above. In other words, because the expectation remedy *in effect* guarantees performance, it does not force *B1* to take into account the fact that the reliance expenditure will be worthless if the contract is breached. It therefore encourages excessive reliance investments.

Under the reliance remedy, *B1* either will receive the widget or be given an amount of money equal to his reliance expenditure plus the contract price. Thus, if the contract is performed, the extra $24 investment in reliance will have been worthwhile because it will have raised the value of the widget by $30. If the contract is breached, the extra $24 will be returned because reliance damages will be that much higher. *B1* therefore will have an incentive to spend the extra $24 on reliance because this expenditure is, in effect, an investment that has no "downside" risk but that does have "upside" potential. In other words, the reliance remedy also encourages excessive reliance expenditures.

Under the restitution remedy, *B1* either will receive the widget or be given an amount of money equal to the contract price. Unlike under the expectation remedy, he is not effectively guaranteed performance, and, unlike under the reliance remedy, he does not get his reliance investment back in the event of breach. *B1*'s reliance expenditure is now, in effect, a risky investment with a positive payoff in the event of performance and a negative payoff in the event of breach. Therefore, in order for *B1* to determine whether it is worthwhile to spend an extra $24 on reliance, he needs to know the probabilities of performance and breach. Suppose *S* breaches only when it is efficient for a breach to occur — that is, only when *B2* values the widget at $250.[21] Given the assumption that the three

21. The supposition that *S* breaches only when it is efficient for a breach to occur is clearly counterfactual in general under the restitution

values *B2* might attach to the widget — $0, $180, and $250 — are all equally likely, there is a two-thirds chance of performance and a one-third chance of breach. Thus, the *expected* benefit to *B1* of the reliance expenditure is $20 — the $30 increase in value of the widget multiplied by the probability of obtaining this value. *B1* will not spend an extra $24 in reliance to obtain this expected benefit. In other words, the restitution remedy leads to the efficient reliance investment.

This discussion of the effects of breach of contract remedies on the reliance decision illustrates several general results. The principal one is that, among the remedies considered, only the restitution remedy induces efficient reliance investments. It does this because it forces the party investing in reliance to take into account the fact that the reliance expenditure is worthless if the contract is breached.[22] The expectation remedy generally leads to too much reliance because it gives the relying party the value that would have been created by the reliance investment if the contract had been performed. The reliance remedy also generally induces excessive reliance because it reimburses the relying party for the cost of reliance in the event of breach.

Another consideration in the economic analysis of breach of contract remedies is the cost of obtaining the information needed to implement each remedy. The expectation remedy requires a court to estimate what the value of the contract would have been to the breached-against party if the contract had been completed. In many contract situations, this value may be very difficult to determine. For example, suppose the buyer is purchasing specialized memory chips for the production of a newly designed home computer. The court would have to predict how profitable the new computer would have been. The restitution and reliance remedies both require knowledge of the contract price, which should be readily avail-

---

remedy. This supposition is used nonetheless because it allows the effect of the restitution remedy on the extent of the reliance investment to be illustrated most easily.

22. The "remedy" of no damages at all also would lead to the efficient reliance investment for the same reason.

able. The reliance remedy also requires information about the breached-against party's reliance expenditures. Since these expenditures will have been made prior to the parties' coming to the court, it should be easier for the court to obtain this information than the information required by the expectation remedy. Thus, in general, the expectation remedy probably would be the most costly to implement, the restitution remedy would be the cheapest, and the reliance remedy would be somewhere in-between.

Note also that if the court incorrectly estimates the value of performance to the breached-against party, then the conclusions regarding the effects of the expectation remedy on the breach decision and on the reliance decision would have to be modified. Similarly, if the breached-against party's reliance expenditures are likely to be incorrectly determined, the conclusions regarding the effects of the reliance remedy also would be different.

The discussion in this chapter has shown that, in general, there does not exist a breach of contract remedy that is efficient with respect to both the breach decision and the reliance decision. With respect to breach, the expectation remedy is ideal, whereas with respect to reliance, the restitution remedy is ideal. Thus, which remedy is best overall depends on whether the breach decision or the reliance decision is more important in terms of efficiency. For example, in the example used in this chapter an inefficient breach occurred when S sold the widget to $B2$ when $B2$'s value was $180. Because $B1$ valued the widget at $200, there was an efficiency loss of $20 from the inefficient breach; assuming this occurs with a one-third chance (the chance that $B2$ values the widget at $180), the expected value of the efficiency loss is $6⅔ (1/3 × $20). Inefficient reliance occurred when $B1$ spent the additional $24 in reliance. Because the expected benefit of reliance only was $20, there was an efficiency loss of $4 from inefficient reliance. Thus, in this example, because the efficiency loss from inefficient breach exceeds the efficiency loss from inefficient reliance, the expectation remedy would be preferred.

A key assumption in the discussion in this chapter was that the parties were neutral with regard to risk. In Chapter 8 we will reconsider breach of contract remedies when the parties are assumed to be averse to risk and see that, in general, none of the remedies discussed here are ideal with respect to risk allocation.

CHAPTER 6

THIRD APPLICATION — AUTOMOBILE ACCIDENTS

In both of the applications discussed thus far — nuisance law and breach of contract — it was appropriate to consider the possibility that bargaining among the parties could lead to the efficient solution. Thus, the framework of the Coase Theorem was directly applicable to these kinds of disputes. In the next application that we will examine — automobile accidents involving pedestrians — bargaining obviously cannot lead to the efficient outcome because neither drivers nor pedestrians know in advance with whom to bargain. The Coase Theorem may be helpful nonetheless. Efficient legal rules for dealing with driver-pedestrian accidents still can be derived by imagining what rules a driver and a pedestrian would have chosen if they could have costlessly gotten together before the accident. As in the other applications, the parties would have agreed to remedies that lead them to behave so as to maximize their joint benefits net of their joint costs.

A simple example will be used to investigate the efficiency of different legal remedies in driver-pedestrian accidents. In this example, it is assumed that drivers and pedestrians are risk neutral; the discussion therefore will be in terms of the *expected* accident cost to a pedestrian — the magnitude of the harm if an accident occurs multiplied by its probability of occurrence. It also is assumed initially that only the speed of drivers affects the pedestrians' expected harm. (The example will be extended later in this chapter to include the possibilities that the number of miles driven or the care exercised by pedestrians also affects the expected harm.) The driver has

TABLE 3

Automobile Accident Example — Driver's Care Affects Expected
Accident Cost

Behavior of Driver	Benefit to Driver	Expected Accident Cost to Pedestrian	Benefit Minus Cost
Drive rapidly	$120	$100	$20
Drive moderately	$80	$40	$40
Drive slowly	$50	$20	$30

three choices: drive rapidly, drive moderately, or drive slowly. Each choice results in some benefit to the driver and some expected accident cost to the pedestrian. The driver's benefit from driving faster might be the dollar value he places on saving time. The pedestrian's harm also is assumed to have a monetary value.[23]

The data for the example are described in Table 3. For each choice of the driver, the table lists the benefit to the driver and the expected accident cost to the pedestrian. The efficient outcome requires that the driver act so as to maximize benefit less cost. Given the data in Table 3, it is efficient for the driver to drive moderately. Relative to this outcome, driving rapidly is inefficient because it increases the pedestrian's expected losses by $60 while increasing the driver's benefits only by $40. And driving slowly is inefficient because it lowers the driver's benefits by $30 while lowering the pedestrian's expected losses only by $20.

The Driver's Care

We will now consider the effects on the driver's behavior of two alternative rules of liability in accident law — *strict*

23. As suggested in note 6 above and in the accompanying text, economic analysis still can be used when the harm is not equivalent to the loss of money (as is the case with pain and suffering). However, the discussion would be more complicated.

liability and *negligence*. Under each, the driver will choose the action that maximizes his benefits net of his expected liability payments. Under the rule of *strict liability*, the driver will be made liable for the pedestrian's accident losses regardless of the driver's care. Thus, for each action, the driver's benefit net of his expected liability payments is the same as the last column in Table 3. The driver therefore will choose to drive moderately — the efficient outcome. In essence, the rule of strict liability results in efficient behavior because it forces the injurer — in this example, the driver — to take into account all of the adverse effects of his behavior on the victim — the pedestrian.

For the rule of strict liability to be efficient, the court generally must be able to obtain correct information about the victim's damages. To see why, suppose in the example that the court estimates damages to be one-half of the victim's actual damages. Then, referring to Table 3, the driver's benefits net of his expected liability payments would be $70 if he drives rapidly ($120 − $50), $60 if he drives moderately ($80 − $20), and $40 if he drives slowly ($50 − $10). He therefore would choose to drive rapidly — faster than is efficient.[24] Similarly, suppose the court estimates damages to be twice what they actually are. Then the driver's benefits net of his expected liability payments would be, respectively, −$80 ($120 − $200), $0 ($80 − $80), and $10 ($50 − $40). Thus, the driver would choose to drive slowly — too slow relative to desired driving behavior. In order to focus on other considerations, it will be assumed hereafter that the court has accurate information about the victim's damages.

Under the rule of *negligence*, the driver will be made liable for the pedestrian's accident losses only if the driver does not meet some standard of care. Suppose this standard is determined by the care that would be taken if the driver acted efficiently. In the example, this corresponds to driving at moderate speed. Thus, the driver would be liable for the pedestrian's

---

24. For analogous reasons, the driver also generally would drive faster than is efficient if, given his income or wealth, he does not expect to be able to pay the full amount of the victim's damages.

accident losses only if the driver chooses to drive rapidly. Therefore, if he drives rapidly his benefit net of his expected liability payments is $20 (a $120 benefit less a $100 expected liability payment). If he drives moderately, it is $80 (just the benefit because there is no liability), and if he drives slowly it is $50 (again, just the benefit). Consequently, under the rule of negligence with this standard of care, the driver will choose the efficient outcome of driving moderately. In essence, the rule of negligence leads to the efficient outcome because the injurer prefers to comply with the standard of care — to avoid having liability increase from zero to the victim's damages if the standard is violated — and the standard is selected to correspond to the desired behavior.

For the rule of negligence to be efficient, it is necessary for the court to have enough information to determine the efficient outcome so that the standard of care can be chosen to correspond to it. To see why, suppose in the example that the court mistakenly believes that it is efficient for the driver to drive slowly and therefore makes this behavior the standard of care. In other words, the driver is liable for the pedestrian's losses if he drives rapidly or moderately, but not if he drives slowly. Then, referring to Table 3, the driver's benefit net of his expected liability payments is $20 if he drives rapidly ($120 − $100), $40 if he drives moderately ($80 − $40), and $50 if he drives slowly ($50 − $0). Thus, the driver would choose to drive slowly, an inefficient outcome. Similarly, if the court were to make the standard of care too lenient rather than too strict, the driver would choose to drive faster than would be efficient. It will be assumed hereafter that the court has enough information to select the standard of care that corresponds to the efficient outcome.

The discussion thus far illustrates a general principle in the economic analysis of accident law: In accident situations in which the only issue is how to induce the injurer to take appropriate care, both strict liability and negligence are efficient, provided that liability equals actual damages if strict liability is used and that the standard of care corresponds to the efficient outcome if negligence is used.

The Pedestrian's Care

In many accident situations, however, the problem is not just to control the injurer's behavior. In general, both the injurer and the victim can affect the probability and the magnitude of the harm. For example, a pedestrian can walk rather than run while crossing a street, or a cyclist can wear a protective helmet. When both the injurer and the victim can affect the expected harm, the issue is how to induce both parties to take appropriate care. We will now reexamine the rules of strict liability and negligence with respect to this additional consideration.

To allow for the expected harm to be determined by the behavior of both the driver and the pedestrian, it is necessary to extend the example used above. It will now be assumed that the pedestrian has one choice — whether to walk or to run. If she walks, then her expected accident loss is $100 if the driver drives rapidly, $40 if the driver drives moderately, and $20 if the driver drives slowly. These are the same values used in Table 3. If the pedestrian runs, her corresponding expected accident losses are $110, $50, and $30. In other words, running is assumed to raise the expected harm by $10 regardless of the driver's behavior.[25] The data for the extended example are summarized in Table 4, where it also is assumed that the driver's benefits from driving are the same as in Table 3.

The efficient solution to the accident problem now involves a specific action both by the driver and by the pedestrian. If the pedestrian walks, the problem is the same as before, and the efficient outcome with respect to the driver's behavior is for him to drive moderately. If the pedestrian runs, Table 4

25. In general, the effect of the pedestrian's care on expected accident losses would depend on the driver's behavior. For example, suppose the pedestrian's decision whether to walk or to run determines the probability of an accident, while the driver's speed determines the magnitude of the harm if an accident occurs. Then the faster the driver drives, the more the expected harm will be raised by the pedestrian's decision to run. The assumption made in the text — that running raises the expected harm by an amount that does not depend on the driver's behavior — greatly simplifies the subsequent analysis without affecting the general conclusions.

TABLE 4

Automobile Accident Example — Driver's Care and Pedestrian's Care Affect Expected Accident Cost

Behavior of Driver	Benefit to Driver	Expected Accident Cost to Pedestrian (Depending on Pedestrian's Behavior)	Benefit Minus Cost (Depending on Pedestrian's Behavior)
Drive rapidly	$120	$100 (walks)	$20 (walks)
		$110 (runs)	$10 (runs)
Drive moderately	$80	$40 (walks)	$40 (walks)
		$50 (runs)	$30 (runs)
Drive slowly	$50	$20 (walks)	$30 (walks)
		$30 (runs)	$20 (runs)

shows that benefits minus costs also are maximized when the driver drives moderately. Thus, regardless of the pedestrian's behavior, the efficient solution involves driving moderately. Whether it is efficient for the pedestrian to walk or to run depends on the relevant costs and benefits. Running rather than walking increases the pedestrian's expected harm by $10 (regardless of the driver's behavior). It will be assumed that running provides additional benefits to the pedestrian valued at $5 — for example, due to the saving of time. Thus, given these costs and benefits, the efficient solution involves the pedestrian walking.[26]

Now reconsider the rule of strict liability. The driver's benefit net of his expected liability payments corresponds to the last column in Table 4. If the pedestrian walks, the relevant values are $20, $40, and $30, depending on whether the driver drives rapidly, moderately, or slowly. The driver therefore

26. For simplicity, the benefit to the pedestrian from running or walking is not included in Table 4. Thus, Table 4 refers solely to the benefits and costs associated with the driver's behavior (which depend in part on the pedestrian's behavior).

would choose to drive moderately. If the pedestrian runs, the corresponding values are $10, $30, and $20, and the driver also would choose to drive moderately. Thus, regardless of the pedestrian's behavior, the rule of strict liability will lead the driver to behave efficiently in this example. However, the rule of strict liability will not be efficient with respect to the pedestrian's behavior. Because the pedestrian will be fully compensated for her losses, she will ignore these losses when deciding whether to walk or to run. She only will consider the $5 extra benefit from running. The pedestrian therefore will choose to run even though running increases expected accident costs by $10.

The problem of controlling the victim's behavior under the rule of strict liability can be solved by adding a defense of *contributory negligence*. Then, the injurer is strictly liable unless the victim is contributorily negligent. This rule will result in the desired behavior of both parties.

To see this in the example, let the standard of care applicable to the pedestrian correspond to the efficient behavior of the pedestrian — walking. Thus, if the pedestrian walks, she is not contributorily negligent, so the driver would be strictly liable. If she runs, she is contributorily negligent, so the driver would be free of liability. The pedestrian then has to bear her own losses. Thus, while running rather than walking provides benefits valued at $5, it increases the expected accident cost borne by the pedestrian from zero to $110, $50, or $30, depending on whether the driver drives rapidly, moderately, or slowly (see Table 4). Clearly, the pedestrian will choose to walk in order to avoid having to bear her own losses. Given this choice by the pedestrian, the driver will be strictly liable. We already have seen that this will lead the driver to choose to drive moderately. Thus, the rule of strict liability with a defense of contributory negligence will cause both parties to take an efficient amount of care.

Next, reconsider the rule of negligence in terms of the incentives it creates for both parties to take appropriate care. Assume, as before, that the driver is negligent only if he drives rapidly. If the pedestrian walks, the driver's benefits net of his expected liability payments are the same as discussed earlier under the negligence rule, so the driver will choose to drive moderately. If the pedestrian runs, the driver's benefits net of his expected liability payments are $10 if he drives rapidly ($120 − $110), $80 if he drives moderately ($80 − $0), and $50 if he drives slowly ($50 − $0). Thus, the driver will choose to drive moderately regardless of what the pedestrian does. Because the driver therefore will not be negligent, the pedestrian will bear her own losses. She will then compare the $5 extra benefit from running to the $10 increase in expected accident costs and will choose to walk. Thus, the rule of negligence will lead both parties to take an efficient amount of care.

Note that under the negligence rule it is not necessary to add a defense of contributory negligence to get the victim to take proper precautions. If a contributory negligence defense were added, it would not affect the conclusion that both parties will take an efficient amount of care. The victim would meet the standard of care applied to her to avoid being contributorily negligent and having to bear her own losses. Given that the victim is not contributorily negligent, the injurer will meet the standard of care applied to him to avoid being negligent and having to compensate the victim for her losses.

The preceding discussion of the accident problem when both parties can affect the expected harm illustrates another general result in the economic analysis of liability rules: In accident situations in which the problem is to induce both the injurer and the victim to take appropriate care, a rule of strict liability with a defense of contributory negligence *or* a rule of negligence — with or without a defense of contributory negligence — is efficient.

The Activity-Level Issue

In many accident situations, expected accident losses depend not only on the care exercised by each party, but also on the extent to which each party participates in the activity that is the source of the dispute. For example, the number of driver-pedestrian accidents depends in part on how much drivers drive and on how frequently pedestrians travel by foot (rather than, say, by bus). The efficient level of participation in the dispute-creating activity is determined by comparing the benefits a party obtains from greater participation — for example, from the more extensive use of one's car — to the resulting increase in expected accident costs. In general, then, the problem to be solved by liability rules is how to induce both parties to take appropriate care *and* to engage in the activity to an appropriate extent.

To examine whether the rules of strict liability and negligence lead to the efficient level of participation in the activity, the simple version of the driver-pedestrian example — in which only the driver's speed affects the pedestrian's expected accident costs — will be extended to include the number of miles driven. (The more general case in which expected losses also are affected by the pedestrian's care and level of participation in the activity will be discussed below.) Now suppose that expected accident costs depend not only on whether the driver drives slowly, moderately, or rapidly, but also on whether he drives "a little" or "a lot." If he drives a little, then the relevant data are assumed to be the same as in the simple version of the example — that is, the same as in Table 3. If he drives a lot, then his benefits are assumed to increase by $20 and the pedestrian's expected accident costs are assumed to rise by $30, regardless of the speed at which he drives.[27] The data for the extended example are summarized in Table 5.

Because the additional benefits from driving a lot are less than the increase in expected accident costs, the efficient solution involves driving a little. If the driver drives only a little, the problem is the same as that discussed in the simple version of the driver-pedestrian example, where it was efficient for the driver to drive at moderate speed. Put differently, driving moderately and only a little maximizes benefits less costs. This can be seen directly in the last column of Table 5.

Under strict liability, the driver's benefit net of his expected liability payments corresponds to the last column in

27. A point analogous to the one made in note 25 above applies here.

TABLE 5

Automobile Accident Example — Driver's Care and Activity Level Affect Expected Accident Cost

Behavior of Driver	Benefit to Driver (Depending on How Much Driver Drives)	Expected Accident Cost to Pedestrian (Depending on How Much Driver Drives)	Benefit Minus Cost (Depending on How Much Driver Drives)
Drive rapidly	$120 (a little)	$100 (a little)	$20 (a little)
	$140 (a lot)	$130 (a lot)	$10 (a lot)
Drive moderately	$80 (a little)	$40 (a little)	$40 (a little)
	$100 (a lot)	$70 (a lot)	$30 (a lot)
Drive slowly	$50 (a little)	$20 (a little)	$30 (a little)
	$70 (a lot)	$50 (a lot)	$20 (a lot)

Table 5. Thus, the driver will choose to drive moderately and only a little. As in the earlier versions of the driver-pedestrian example, strict liability leads the injurer to behave efficiently because it forces him to take into account the adverse effects of his behavior on the victim. The only difference now is that one relevant aspect of his behavior is the extent of his participation in the activity.

Under negligence, suppose, as in the earlier versions of the example, that the driver is negligent only if he drives rapidly. Then, if his participation in the activity corresponds to driving a little, his benefit net of his expected liability payment is $20 ($120 − $100) if he drives rapidly, $80 ($80 − $0) if he drives moderately, and $50 ($50 − $0) if he drives slowly. If he drives a lot, the comparable values are $10 ($140 − $130) if he drives rapidly, $100 ($100 − $0) if he drives moderately, and $70 ($70 − $0) if he drives slowly. The driver therefore will choose to drive a lot and to drive at moderate speed. In other words, the negligence rule with this standard of care is efficient with respect to the injurer's care but not with respect to his level of participation in the activity.

Recall from the discussion of the negligence rule in the simple version of the driver-pedestrian example that this rule is efficient only if the standard of care corresponds to the efficient behavior of the injurer.[28] The negligence rule is not efficient in the present version of the example precisely because the standard of care does not take into account one relevant aspect of the injurer's behavior — the extent of his participation in the activity. If the standard of care were to correspond to the efficient outcome of driving moderately and only a little — so that the driver *would* be negligent if he drives a lot even if he drives moderately — then the negligence rule also would lead to the efficient outcome.

In practice, however, it often is not feasible to include the level of participation in the activity as an aspect of the standard of care. For example, it would be virtually impossible for a court to determine how many miles a particular person drives each year since that person might drive a car that is shared with other family members or he might drive different cars owned by the household. If the injurer's level of participation in the activity is omitted from the standard of care, then a negligence rule generally will lead him to participate in the activity to an excessive degree. The reason for this is straightforward. If the care he exercises meets the standard of care, he will not be liable for any damages. Therefore, in deciding how much to participate in the activity, he will consider the additional benefits from greater participation but not the increase in expected accident costs. This problem with the negligence rule was illustrated by the driver-pedestrian example. Given a standard of care based only on the driver's speed, the driver chose to meet the standard by driving moderately. But he also chose to drive a lot, exceeding the efficient level of participation in the activity.

The discussion thus far of the activity-level issue can be summarized as follows: In accident situations in which the problem is to induce the injurer both to take appropriate care and to participate in the activity at an appropriate level, strict liability is efficient. Negligence also is efficient if the standard

28. See pp. 45-46 above.

of care encompasses both the injurer's care and his level of participation in the activity. However, if the standard does not include the injurer's activity level, then the negligence rule will lead to excessive participation in the activity. In practice, the negligence rule is likely to be inefficient for this reason.

In some accident situations, the expected accident losses may depend not only on the injurer's care and activity level, but also on the victim's care and activity level. In this more general setting, results analogous to those just discussed would occur. Strict liability with a defense of contributory negligence would be efficient if the standard of care applicable to the victim encompasses both the victim's care and her activity level. However, if it includes only her care, then the victim will engage in the activity to an excessive degree. Similarly, negligence would be efficient if the standard of care applicable to the injurer includes both aspects of his behavior. If it includes only his care, then he will participate in the activity too much. Thus, if it is not feasible to include either party's activity level in the standard of care, the preferred liability rule depends on whether it is more important to control the injurer's or the victim's activity level. If the injurer's activity level is of greater concern, then strict liability with a defense of contributory negligence should be used. If the victim's activity level is more important, then negligence is preferable.

The final consideration in the economic analysis of liability rules that will be discussed in this chapter is the effect of each rule on the administrative costs of resolving accident disputes. These costs depend both on the number of cases litigated and on the cost of resolving each case.[29] The negligence rule would be expected to generate less litigation than the strict liability rule for the following reason. Consider the negligence rule in an accident situation in which the injurer's care was very likely to have satisfied the standard of care.

---

29. Although the following discussion is concerned with disputes that are litigated, similar points could be made with respect to disputes that are settled after costly negotiation.

Given the cost to the victim of litigating, she might not find it worthwhile to bring an action against the injurer because of the low probability of success. Yet, under the strict liability rule, she might be willing to bring an action in this accident situation because the injurer's care is not a bar to a successful suit.

Although there may be fewer cases under the negligence rule, the administrative cost of resolving each case may well be higher than under the strict liability rule. The justification for this conclusion is easiest to see when the only problem is to induce the injurer to take appropriate care. To apply a strict liability rule, the court needs to know the victim's damages. But to apply a negligence rule, the court needs to know not only the victim's damages and the injurer's benefits at different levels of the injurer's care — in order to choose a standard of care that corresponds to the efficient outcome — but also how the injurer behaved — in order to determine whether he met the standard. (When the problem is to induce both the injurer and the victim to take appropriate care, this argument does not apply because the strict liability rule then requires a defense of contributory negligence to be efficient.)

On balance, therefore, administrative cost considerations do not clearly favor either rule. While the negligence rule is likely to lead to fewer cases being litigated than the strict liability rule, it may well generate higher administrative costs in each case.

This chapter has shown that in accident situations in which the only problem is to create incentives for the parties to take appropriate care, both strict liability with a defense of contributory negligence and negligence are efficient. If the problem also is to induce the parties to engage in the dispute-creating activity to an appropriate extent, then both rules still are efficient provided that the relevant standards of care — the victim's under the contributory negligence defense and the injurer's under the negligence rule — incorporate the activity-level decision of the party to whom the standard applies. In practice, however, this is not likely to be feasible. If the standard of care refers only to the relevant party's level of care, then strict liability with a defense of contributory negligence will lead to excessive participation in the activity by the victim, and negligence will lead to excessive participation by the injurer. In many accident situations it may be apparent that one party's activity level matters more than the other's, in which case the superiority of one of the rules will be clear.

An important assumption in the discussion in this chapter was that both drivers and pedestrians were risk neutral. When accident law is reconsidered in Chapter 9 under the assumption of risk aversion, it will be seen that strict liability and negligence may no longer be efficient even in accident situations in which only the injurer's care determines the victim's expected losses.

CHAPTER 7

RISK BEARING AND INSURANCE

In both the breach of contract and automobile accident applications, some sort of risk was present. In the contract example, there was uncertainty about the needs of the second buyer; and in the accident example, there was, implicitly, uncertainty regarding whether an accident would occur. Because of the assumption in both cases that the parties were risk neutral, risk per se did not matter.

We will now consider the generally more realistic assumption that parties are *risk averse* (at least with respect to large risks). This means that they care not only about the expected value of a risky situation, but also about the absolute magnitude of the risk. For example, a risk-averse person, unlike a risk-neutral person, would not be indifferent between the certainty of winning $5,000 and a 50 percent chance of winning $10,000. The risk-averse person would, by definition, prefer $5,000 with certainty.[30]

The Bearing of Risk

To see the value of reducing or eliminating the risk borne by risk-averse persons, consider the following situation. Suppose you have recently graduated from law school and have become an associate in a private law firm. Your first assign-

---

30. Individuals may also be risk preferring. In the example in the text, this would mean that they would prefer a 50 percent chance of winning $10,000 to the certainty of winning $5,000. This case will not be dealt with in the book.

ment is to work full-time on a case that the firm has accepted on a *contingent fee* basis — the firm will receive $200,000 at the end of the year if it wins the case and nothing otherwise. Your employer knows from previous experience that there is a 50 percent chance of winning the case. The firm proposes to pay you $200,000 for the year if you win and nothing if you lose, so your expected salary is $100,000. How much would you be willing to accept with certainty instead? Suppose you would accept as little as $80,000 to avoid being subjected to the risk.

This situation provides a nice business opportunity for me. I am going to start a business with some friends in which we will bear the risks of income fluctuations of recent law school graduates who work on contingent fee cases. Here's our deal: We will pay you $90,000 with certainty if you assign to us the claim on the law firm you are working for. Suppose this deal attracts one hundred other lawyers in circumstances similar to yours. At the end of the year, we can count on approximately fifty of our claims to pay $200,000 and the rest nothing, so our expected revenue is $10 million. Because we have to pay one hundred lawyers $90,000 each, our costs are $9 million. Thus, our profits will be approximately $1 million. We are better off entering into this deal — although each of us is risk averse too, our risks are minimal since we can be confident that approximately fifty of our claims will pay off.[31] You are better off under this deal too — you were willing to accept as little as $80,000 to avoid the risk, but you have received $90,000. Therefore, this agreement between us — which is a form of insurance — is efficient.

If it isn't already obvious, we should now identify ourselves. We are the partners in your law firm. The partners bear the risks of the firm's successes and failures, while the associates' incomes are guaranteed. This makes sense because the partners can better bear the risks of the firm — they can

---

31. Readers familiar with the basic principles of probability theory will recognize that the conclusion that our risks are minimal does not follow without some additional assumptions. It is sufficient to assume that the outcomes of the associates' cases are "independent" (in the technical statistical sense) and that each of our shares in the business is "small."

"average out" the results of many risky cases and, because they have more wealth, they can better absorb the risks that remain.[32]

The preceding discussion has been about a *beneficial risk* — that is, a risk that someone would accept voluntarily. For such risks, a risk-averse person is willing to settle for less than the expected value of the risk. In the law firm example, rather than accept the risk of an equal chance of getting $200,000 or nothing, with an expected benefit of $100,000, the associate was willing to accept as little as $80,000 with certainty. Similarly, for a *detrimental risk* — a risk that someone would not accept voluntarily — a risk-averse person would be willing to pay more than the expected value of the risk to avoid it. For example, consider a risk involving an equal chance of losing $200,000 or nothing, thus having an expected loss of $100,000. A risk-averse person might be willing to pay as much as $130,000 to avoid this risk.

Because risk-averse individuals are willing to pay for the reduction of risk, just as they are willing to pay for more tangible commodities, the benefit from eliminating or reducing the risk borne by such individuals is properly included in the efficiency calculus. For a beneficial risk, a natural way to measure the benefit from eliminating risk is to compare the expected value of the risk and the least amount of money the person would accept with certainty instead. In the law firm example, the expected value of the risk was $100,000, while the associate was willing to accept as little as $80,000 with certainty. Thus, the benefit from removing the risk was $20,000. Similarly, for a detrimental risk, the benefit from eliminating risk can be measured by the difference between the expected value of the risk and the greatest amount of money the person would pay to avoid the risk. Thus, in the detrimental risk example at the end of the previous paragraph, the benefit from removing the risk would be $30,000 because

---

32. This statement obviously presumes that the higher a person's wealth, the less averse he is to a given size risk. This is a standard assumption in the economic analysis of risk.

the risk-averse person was willing to pay $130,000 to avoid a risk that had an expected loss of $100,000.

Insurance

One common way of eliminating risk is through insurance. For detrimental risks, the insured person pays some amount of money with certainty — the insurance premium — in return for which he is fully compensated if the undesirable risk materializes. For beneficial risks, the insured person receives some amount of money with certainty in return for allowing someone else to benefit from the desirable outcome if it occurs, as in the law firm example. This too may be thought of as a form of insurance.

An insurance policy that completely eliminates risk might, however, have an undesirable side effect. In the law firm example, the associate will have less of an incentive to work hard in order to win the case if her income for the year does not depend on her winning the case. This kind of problem also arises with respect to undesirable risks. For example, if personal items left in your car are completely insured against theft, you may be more likely to leave your camera on the back seat rather than to go to the trouble of putting it in the trunk. These two examples illustrate a general problem — the provision of insurance may increase the probability of a loss or the size of the loss because the insured person has less of an incentive to take precautions. This phenomenon is referred to in the insurance literature as the problem of *moral hazard*.

In principle, the moral hazard problem can be overcome by adjusting the insurance premium to reflect the increase in the expected loss resulting from the insured person's taking less care. For example, suppose your camera is worth $500 and that putting it in the trunk of your car eliminates the possibility of theft, whereas leaving it on the back seat leads to a one-in-a-hundred chance of having it stolen. In other words, leaving it on the back seat results in an *expected* loss of $5. If your insurance premium were to increase by $5 if you regularly left your camera on the back seat of your car, then you would leave it there only if it is worth at least $5 to you to do so. It may or may not be worth this much to leave it there. For example, if you are a professional photographer specializing in outdoor photography, it probably would be worth paying $5 more for the extra convenience, whereas for most people the added convenience would not be worth this much. In either case, by being forced to pay more because of the increased expected loss, the insured person will have the appropriate incentive to take precautions. In other words, the moral hazard problem can be eliminated if the insurance premium depends on how much care is exercised by the insured person.

This solution to the moral hazard problem often is not feasible in practice because the insurer cannot cheaply monitor the behavior of the person being insured. In the camera example, to decide whether to raise the premium by $5, the insurance company would have to determine whether the insured person regularly left his camera on the back seat of his car. In the law firm example, monitoring of associates' effort is easier, and, as a result, bonuses and promotions can be used to some extent to encourage appropriate effort.

There are other alternatives to monitoring the insured person's behavior and adjusting the premium accordingly. In general, these involve providing only partial insurance coverage in order to induce the insured person to take some precautions. Sometimes this partial coverage takes the form of a *deductible*, in which, for example, the insured person bears the first $100 of loss and the insurance company bears the rest. Other times partial coverage takes the form of *co-insurance*, in which, for example, the insured person bears 20 percent of all losses. In either case, this approach is obviously a compromise because it leaves some risk on a risk-averse person and it will not completely solve the problem of moral hazard. On balance, however, partial insurance may be preferable both to no insurance at all (which leaves the most risk on risk-averse persons) and to complete insurance (which provides little or no incentive to take precautions).

The discussion in this chapter has shown that the elimination or reduction of risk borne by a risk-averse person is a benefit that should be taken into account in applying the efficiency criterion. One common way in which risk is reduced is through insurance. An ideal insurance policy has two features — it provides full coverage in order to eliminate the bearing of risk, and it bases the premium on the behavior of the insured person in order to avoid the problem of moral hazard. In practice, however, monitoring the insured person's behavior often is difficult; consequently, only partial insurance coverage may be provided in order to increase the insured person's incentive to take precautions.

We will now return to the breach of contract and automobile accident applications and reexamine them in the light of these principles of risk bearing and insurance. The contract application illustrates the case of a beneficial risk (uncertainty about a higher third-party offer), while the accident application obviously represents the case of a detrimental risk.

CHAPTER 8

FOURTH APPLICATION —
BREACH OF CONTRACT AGAIN

In the discussion of breaches of contracts in Chapter 5, it was assumed that the parties were risk neutral. The primary conclusions there were that the expectation remedy was most efficient with respect to the breach decision and that the restitution remedy was most efficient with respect to the reliance decision. We will now reexamine breach of contract remedies when at least one of the parties is risk averse. In order to focus on the risk-allocation issue, assumptions will be made that imply that both the breach decision and the reliance decision will be efficient under all of the remedies considered.

The analysis will be undertaken using a variation of the earlier example of a seller S, who can produce a widget for $150, an initial buyer $B1$, who values the widget at $200 and who has to make a reliance investment of $10, and a possible second buyer $B2$. The contract price agreed to by S and $B1$ is again payable in advance.[33] It is assumed in this chapter that $B1$'s reliance expenditure is fixed, so there cannot be a problem of inefficient reliance. It is also assumed that the value $B2$ attaches to the widget is either $0 or $250. The facts of this example are summarized in Table 6 (which is a slightly modified version of Table 2).

By eliminating the possibility considered earlier that $B2$'s value might be $180, the problem of inefficient breach is

---

33. Although none of the results in this chapter depend on the specific contract price, it will be useful to keep in mind that the contract price varies with the damage payment for the reasons discussed in Chapter 5. See pp. 32-33 above.

TABLE 6

Breach of Contract Example

S is the seller:

    S's cost to produce the widget is $150.

B1 is the initial buyer:

    B1 values the widget at $200.

    B1's reliance expenditure is $10.

    B1 pays *S* the contract price in advance.

B2 is the second buyer:

    B2 values the widget at $0 or $250.

avoided under all of the remedies examined; this can be explained as follows. It was shown in Chapter 5 that the level of damages under the remedies considered was at least as large as the contract price (this was the level of damages under the restitution remedy), but no greater than the $200 value *B1* attaches to the widget (the level of damages under the expectation remedy).[34] Consequently, if *B2* does not need the widget, *S* obviously will not breach, while if *B2*'s offer is $250, *S* will breach in order to sell to *B2* *regardless of which remedy is used.* In other words, the breach decision will be efficient under all of the remedies considered. Thus, since the reliance expenditure is fixed and the breach decision is efficient, the only issue to be discussed is risk allocation.

Optimal Risk Allocation

Because it will be assumed throughout this chapter that private insurance is not available to the parties, the allocation of contract risks will be determined solely by the remedy for breach of contract. Before examining the effects of different remedies, it will be useful to determine the level of damages

34. See pp. 33-35 above.

that would be awarded in the widget example if the risk were allocated efficiently or optimally. Suppose for a start that the buyer B1 is risk averse and that the seller S is risk neutral.[35] Then, because it is desirable to eliminate the risks imposed on risk-averse persons, B1 should, in effect, be insured and S should bear all of the risk. This can be accomplished by making S pay B1 in the event of a breach an amount of money equal to the value B1 attaches to the widget — that is, $200. Given this damage payment, B1's profit equals his $200 benefit less the contract price and less his $10 reliance expenditure regardless of whether B2's offer materializes and S breaches. S's profit, however, does depend on whether B2's offer occurs. If the offer does not occur, S's profit equals the contract price less his $150 production cost, whereas if the offer does occur, his profit is augmented by $50 — the difference between B2's $250 offer and the $200 damage payment to B1. Thus, with this damage payment, B1 does not bear any risk but S does.

Now suppose that S is risk averse and B1 is risk neutral. Then S should be insured and all of the risk should be borne by B1. This can be achieved by making S pay B1, if a breach occurs, an amount of money equal to B2's offer — that is, $250. S's profit then equals the contract price less his $150 production cost regardless of whether the contract is performed or breached because, in the event of a breach, he must disgorge the extra profits he otherwise would have obtained from the sale to B2. B1's profit equals his $200 value less the contract price and less his $10 reliance expenditure if the contract is performed, or the $250 damage payment less the contract price and reliance expenditure if the contract is breached. Thus, only B1's profit is uncertain.

Finally, if both B1 and S are risk averse, the risk should be shared between them in a way that reflects their relative aversion to risk. This can be accomplished by a damage payment between the two extremes discussed above — that is,

35. Recall from note 19 above that B2 is assumed to offer an amount equal to the value he attaches to the widget, so his profits do not depend on how valuable the widget is to him. In other words, B2 does not bear any risk. This is why it does not matter in the example whether B2 is risk neutral or risk averse.

between *B1*'s value of $200 and *B2*'s offer of $250. To the extent that the damage payment is above $200, *B1* bears the risk of a higher offer because the difference between *B1*'s profit when the contract is performed and *B1*'s profit when the contract is breached increases. Similarly, to the extent that the damage payment is below $250, *S* bears this risk because *S*'s profit becomes more uncertain. Thus, the more risk averse *B1* is relative to *S*, the lower the optimal damage payment. Note, however, that the optimal damage payment is never below the $200 value *B1* attaches to the widget. It equals this value only when *B1* is risk averse and *S* is risk neutral.

The Effects of the Remedies

We can now reexamine the expectation, reliance, and restitution remedies to see whether, and under what circumstances, they optimally allocate the contract risks in the example. Under the expectation remedy, if the seller breaches, the buyer can recover from the seller an amount of money that puts the buyer in the same position he would have been in had the contract been completed. As seen in Chapter 5, this corresponds in the example to a damage payment equal to the $200 value *B1* attaches to the widget.[36] *B1*'s profit therefore does not depend on whether *S* breaches to sell the widget to *B2*, but *S*'s profit does. In other words, the beneficial risk of *B2*'s offer is borne entirely by *S*; *B1* is in effect completely insured against this risk. Based on the earlier discussion of optimal risk allocation, we can conclude, therefore, that the expectation remedy is efficient in terms of risk allocation only if the seller is risk neutral and the buyer is risk averse.

Under the reliance remedy, the buyer can recover an amount of money that puts him in the same position he would have been in had he never entered into the contract with the seller. It was seen in Chapter 5 that reliance damages correspond in the example to *B1*'s $10 reliance expenditure plus the contract price; it also was demonstrated that this

36. See pp. 33-34 above.

level of damages was less than the level of expectation damages — that is, less than the $200 value *B1* attaches to the widget.[37] Recall from the discussion of optimal risk allocation earlier in this chapter that the optimal damage payment never is below the $200 value *B1* attaches to the widget and that it is only this low when *B1* is risk averse and *S* is risk neutral. Thus, the reliance remedy never leads to the optimal allocation of the contract risk in this example. Intuitively, this is because the effect of the reliance remedy is to accentuate the risk created by the possibility of a third-party offer. The further the damage payment falls below *B1*'s value of the widget, the greater the variability of both *B1*'s profit and *S*'s profit.

Under the restitution remedy, the buyer can recover any benefit that he has conferred on the seller. It was shown in Chapter 5 that restitution damages correspond in the example to the contract price, which will be below *B1*'s $200 value.[38] Thus, the restitution remedy, like the reliance remedy, never would optimally allocate the contract risk because the damage payment always would be too low.

The preceding discussion illustrates a general conclusion about the risk-allocation effects of breach of contract remedies: When the contract risk is due to the possibility of a third-party offer, the expectation remedy is ideal if the buyer is risk averse and the seller is risk neutral. Moreover, it is preferable to both the reliance and the restitution remedies (regardless of the parties' relative aversion to risk).

In many contract situations, however, the seller may be risk averse and the buyer may be risk neutral, in which case the parties would want the buyer to bear the risk; or both parties may be risk averse, in which case they would want to share the risk rather than to allocate it entirely to one party. Then the expectation remedy is not ideal. However, there is an alternative — a *liquidated damage* remedy — that can allocate the contract risk between the parties in any way they desire. Under a liquidated damage remedy, if the seller breaches, the buyer can recover an amount of money agreed

37. See pp. 34-35 above.
38. See p. 35 above.

to by the parties in advance. This remedy differs from the others in that it is chosen by the parties themselves rather than imposed upon them by a court. If their only concern is with the allocation of risk, as we are assuming in this chapter, then they would choose a damage payment that allocates the risk according to their relative aversion to risk. In principle, then, a liquidated damage remedy always would allocate the contract risk optimally because the liquidated damage payment would equal the optimal damage payment.[39]

To see how a liquidated damage remedy allocates contract risks, suppose in the example that *S* and *B1* are equally risk averse and therefore want to split the beneficial risk of a higher offer from *B2*. This can be done by the completely specified contract discussed in Chapter 5, which had the following provisions. *B1* pays *S* the contract price of $175 in advance. If *B2*'s needs do not materialize, then *S* is to deliver the widget to *B1*. If *B2* does need the widget, then *S* is to sell the widget to *B2* (for $250) rather than to *B1* but then must pay *B1* *liquidated damages* of $225. Under this arrangement, *S*'s profit is $25 if *B2* does not need the widget ($175 − $150) and $50 if *B2* does need it ($175 − $150 + $250 − $225). Similarly, *B1*'s profit is $15 if *B2* does not need the widget ($200 − $175 − $10, where the last item is *B1*'s reliance expenditure) and $40 if *B2* does need it ($225 − $175 − $10). Note that the joint profits of *S* and *B1* rise by $50 if *B2* needs the widget — from joint profits of $40 ($25 + $15) if *B2* does not need the widget to joint profits of $90 ($50 + $40) if he does. The liquidated damage remedy allocates half of this beneficial risk to each party — both *S*'s and *B1*'s profits rise by $25 if *B2* needs the widget. In contrast, the expectation remedy would allocate all of the risk to *S* — *S*'s profit would rise by $50 if *B2* needs the widget whereas *B1*'s profit would not change.

This example illustrates a more general point: A liquidated damage remedy can allocate the contract risks between the

---

39. In practice, however, courts generally will not enforce a liquidated damage agreement unless the liquidated damage payment is a reasonable approximation of the expectation measure of damages. If the liquidated damage payment is larger, it is said to be an unenforceable "penalty."

parties according to their relative aversion to risk. Thus, in terms of risk allocation, a liquidated damage remedy is equivalent to the expectation remedy when the buyer is risk averse and the seller is risk neutral, and it is preferable to the expectation remedy when the opposite is true or when both parties are risk averse. Note, however, that a liquidated damage remedy requires additional negotiation by the parties when they enter into the contract because they must also decide on the amount of the payment in the event of a breach. Thus, the potential benefits of a liquidated damage remedy in terms of risk allocation must be balanced against the additional cost of contract negotiation. If the risk allocation benefits do not justify incurring this extra cost, then a court-imposed remedy, such as the expectation remedy, would be preferable.

The discussion in this chapter reinforces the conclusion in Chapter 5 that there does not exist a breach of contract remedy that is efficient with respect to every consideration. It was shown there that the expectation remedy is preferred with respect to the breach decision and that the restitution remedy is preferred with respect to the reliance decision. And we have seen here that a liquidated damage remedy generally is preferred with respect to risk allocation. Thus, which remedy is best overall depends on the relative importance of these three considerations in a particular type of contract situation.

It may be apparent, however, that one remedy clearly dominates the others in some contractual settings. For example, consider contracts in which the sellers of a good are large companies and the buyers are individuals. Then it might be presumed that the sellers are risk neutral and the buyers are risk averse. Suppose also that the buyers do not have to undertake any reliance investments prior to receiving the good. Then the expectation remedy would be ideal in these types of contracts. It would induce efficient breach decisions by the sellers, allocate the contract risks to a risk-neutral party, and not distort the buyer's reliance decision.

CHAPTER 9

FIFTH APPLICATION —
AUTOMOBILE ACCIDENTS
AGAIN

In the earlier discussion of automobile accidents, it was assumed that the injurer (the driver) and the victim (the pedestrian) were neutral with respect to risk. One of the principal conclusions there was that both strict liability and negligence are efficient if the only problem is to induce the injurer to take appropriate care. We now will reexamine these remedies when the parties are averse to risk. We also will consider the relevance of insurance to the accident problem. If risk allocation is a consideration, it no longer will be true that both liability rules are efficient even when the only other issue is the control of the injurer's care.

The discussion will be based on the simple version of the driver-pedestrian example described in Chapter 6 — in which the victim's expected harm is determined solely by the driver's speed. (To consider the possibility that the driver's activity level or the victim's care or activity level also can affect the expected harm would greatly complicate the discussion of the interaction among liability rules, risk allocation, and insurance without adding much additional insight.) The data for the simple version of the driver-pedestrian example were contained in Table 3, which is reproduced here as Table 7. Table 3 included the *expected* accident cost to the pedestrian but did not explain how it was derived from the underlying probability and magnitude of the loss. This omission was irrelevant because it was assumed that the parties were risk neutral; by

TABLE 7

**Automobile Accident Example — Driver's Care Affects
Expected Accident Cost**

Behavior of Driver	Benefit to Driver	Expected Accident Cost to Pedestrian	Benefit Minus Cost
Drive rapidly	$120	$100	$20
		($= 1/100 \times \$10,000$)	
Drive moderately	$80	$40	$40
		($= 1/250 \times \$10,000$)	
Drive slowly	$50	$20	$30
		($= 1/500 \times \$10,000$)	

definition, they cared only about the expected outcome. Now, however, given the assumption that they are risk averse, not only does the expected value of the loss matter, but so does the particular probability and magnitude of the loss. Suppose, for concreteness, that the loss if an accident occurs is $10,000[40] and that the probability of an accident is 1/100 if the driver drives rapidly, 1/250 if he drives moderately, and 1/500 if he drives slowly. These numbers are included in Table 7 below the expected accident cost data.

Private Insurance Not Available

We will first consider the accident problem when private insurance is not available to either party. This assumption may be realistic in some circumstances. For example, because of the administrative cost of operating an insurance company, the premium charged might have to be so high that risk-averse persons would not be willing to buy insurance at that price.

40. Recall the assumption that all losses are monetary. But see note 23 above.

Consequently, no company would be able to remain in business.

Because we are assuming that just the driver's behavior affects the expected accident loss, only the rules of strict liability and negligence need to be considered. Under strict liability, although neither party can buy private insurance, the pedestrian is in effect insured because, whenever an accident occurs, the driver must compensate the pedestrian for her full damages of $10,000. Thus, under this rule, the risk of an accident is borne entirely by the driver.[41]

Under the rule of negligence, the driver will be liable only if he does not meet the standard of care. Assuming that he does meet it — for the reasons discussed in Chapter 6[42] — he will not be liable and therefore the pedestrian will have to bear her own losses. Thus, under the negligence rule, the risk of an accident is borne entirely by the pedestrian.

This discussion shows that the rules of strict liability and negligence allocate accident risks in completely opposite ways. These risk-allocation effects did not matter in terms of efficiency in our initial discussion of automobile accidents in Chapter 6 because both parties were assumed to be risk neutral. If, however, one party is risk averse and the other is risk neutral, then there is a clear preference for one liability rule. When the pedestrian is the risk-averse party, the rule of strict liability leads to the ideal allocation of risks, whereas if the driver is the risk-averse party, the rule of negligence results in ideal risk allocation.

In many accident situations, however, both parties may be risk averse. It then would be desirable in terms of risk allocation to share the risks rather than, as under the strict liability and negligence rules, to allocate them entirely to one party. This can be accomplished by modifying the strict liability rule. Instead of setting the driver's liability equal to the pedestrian's loss, as is usually done under strict liability, liabil-

41. This statement obviously presumes that the driver has adequate resources with which to compensate the pedestrian. If he does not, then some of the risk will remain on the pedestrian.
42. See pp. 45-46 above.

ity can be set lower than the actual loss, thereby leaving some of the accident risk on the pedestrian. For example, suppose that the driver and the pedestrian are equally risk averse, so that the optimal allocation of the risk would be to share it equally. This allocation will result under strict liability if the driver is made liable for one-half of the pedestrian's loss — $5,000 rather than $10,000 — every time an accident occurs. Clearly, any other allocation of the risk between the two parties can be achieved by setting the level of liability somewhere between zero and the pedestrian's actual loss. Recall from Chapter 6, however, that if liability is less than the pedestrian's actual damages, the driver generally will take less than the efficient amount of care.[43] Thus, if both parties are risk averse and insurance is not available, there may be a tradeoff between the desired allocation of the risk and the desired behavior of the driver.

Ideal Insurance Available

Although the discussion in the preceding paragraph showed that a given accident risk sometimes can be allocated best by a version of strict liability, this outcome is less desirable than removing the risk from the parties altogether, as by private insurance. We will now consider the accident problem when *ideal* private insurance is available to both parties — liability insurance to the driver and first-party accident insurance to the pedestrian. Recall from Chapter 7 that an ideal insurance policy provides full coverage in order to remove all risk from the insured person; it also charges that person a premium for the insurance that reflects the expected losses resulting from his behavior, to avoid the so-called moral hazard problem.[44]

Under the strict liability rule, the pedestrian does not need to purchase insurance because she is in effect insured by the driver. The driver, however, will purchase a liability insurance

43. See p. 46 above.
44. See pp. 60-61 above.

policy with complete coverage. The insurance company's expected payout to the driver equals the driver's expected liability payments, which are determined by the driver's behavior. Thus, given the data in Table 7, the premium charged by the insurance company will be $100 if the driver drives rapidly, $40 if he drives moderately, and $20 if he drives slowly.[45] Confronted with this premium structure the driver will choose to drive moderately because, relative to this choice, driving rapidly leads to a $60 increase in his insurance premium but only to a $40 increase in his benefits, and driving slowly lowers his benefits by $30 while only lowering his insurance premium by $20 (see Table 7). Thus, strict liability combined with ideal insurance is efficient both with respect to the care exercised by the driver and the removal of risk from both parties.

Under the negligence rule, the driver would want to buy liability insurance only if he chooses to drive rapidly, because he would not be liable otherwise.[46] The liability insurer would charge the driver a premium of $100 in these circumstances. Faced with this premium if he drives rapidly and no liability otherwise, the driver will choose to drive moderately because the cost of the insurance policy exceeds the extra benefits from driving rapidly. Thus, the pedestrian will bear her own losses and will purchase a first-party accident insurance policy with full coverage. Given the driver's decision to drive moderately, the pedestrian's expected accident loss is $40, so this will be the premium charged. Because the pedestrian is assumed not to be able to affect the probability or magnitude of the harm, there is no possibility of moral hazard. Thus, negligence combined with ideal insurance also is efficient both with respect to the care exercised and the removal of risk.

45. This statement implicitly assumes that there are no administrative costs of operating the insurance company, and that the company just breaks even — that is, has enough premium revenue to just cover its claim payouts. The break-even assumption would be appropriate, for example, if the insurance industry is competitive and in long-run equilibrium; see pp. 103-105 below.

46. In practice, of course, drivers purchase liability insurance even when they act carefully because there is always the possibility that they will be found negligent by mistake. To take this consideration into account in the text would unnecessarily complicate the analysis.

Imperfect Insurance Available

The preceding analysis showed that when ideal insurance is available, it does not matter whether strict liability or negligence is used in the example under consideration. However, for reasons discussed in Chapter 7, it is not realistic in many, if not most, circumstances to assume that ideal insurance is available: Because of the difficulty or impossibility of monitoring the insured person's behavior, the insurance premium will not respond completely to changes in that behavior. As a result, the insured person will not have an adequate incentive to take precautions that reduce the expected losses. This is the problem of moral hazard. Consequently, the insurance policy may not provide full coverage in order to induce the insured person to take more care. We will therefore complete the discussion of the accident problem by considering the optimal choice of a liability rule when insurance is imperfect because of the moral hazard problem. For simplicity, it will be assumed that the insurer cannot observe the insured person's behavior at all.[47]

Under the rule of strict liability, the driver will want to purchase liability insurance. If the policy provides complete coverage, the driver will not have any incentive to take care because, by assumption, the premium cannot be made to depend on the driver's care. Thus, the driver would choose to drive rapidly. Alternatively, the policy may provide less than full coverage to create some incentive for the driver to drive more slowly. In either case, an ideal outcome will not be achieved under the rule of strict liability. If the coverage is complete, the driver will not exercise appropriate care, and if

---

47. Because individuals who take less care are more likely to have accidents, an insurance company indirectly can obtain some information about the insured person's behavior from the number of claims submitted. (If the premium charged depends on the number of claims previously paid, the policy is said to be "experience rated.") There also may be some ways to directly monitor the insured person's behavior. For example, many companies providing automobile insurance request information about the number of miles driven annually.

the coverage is incomplete, he will bear some risk (and generally still will not take enough care).

Under the negligence rule, the driver will want liability insurance only if he chooses to drive rapidly because he would not be liable for the pedestrian's damages otherwise. If he drives rapidly, the insurance premium would be $100. Given this premium if he drives rapidly and no liability otherwise, the driver will choose to drive moderately. Note that this is the outcome that occurred when ideal insurance was assumed to be available. The fact that the liability insurer now cannot monitor the driver's care is irrelevant because the driver will meet the standard of care and therefore will not be liable.[48] Given the driver's behavior, the pedestrian will bear her own losses and will want a first-party accident insurance policy with full coverage. Because, by assumption, there is nothing the pedestrian can do to affect the probability or magnitude of the loss, there is no moral hazard problem and therefore no reason to deny full coverage to the pedestrian. Thus, under the negligence rule, the driver will exercise appropriate care and bear no risk, and the pedestrian will be fully insured — the efficient solution. In summary, when there is a moral hazard problem with respect to the injurer's behavior but not with respect to the victim's behavior, the negligence rule is preferable to the strict liability rule.

The discussion in this chapter has shown that considerations of risk allocation may provide a reason for adopting one automobile accident remedy rather than another. For example, if insurance is not available, we saw in the simple version of the driver-pedestrian example that the strict liability rule is preferred when the victim is risk averse and the injurer is risk

48. This argument implicitly assumes that, although the insurance company cannot monitor the driver's care before an accident, the court, in applying the negligence rule, can determine the driver's care after an accident. It might be asked then why the insurance company cannot also determine the driver's care *after* an accident. If the company could, this would not affect the discussion in the text because the driver will not need insurance, given his decision to drive moderately.

neutral, and that the negligence rule is superior when the opposite is true. A modification of the strict liability rule — with liability less than the victim's actual loss — is best with respect to risk allocation when both parties are risk averse, but it generally will lead the injurer to take too little care. If ideal insurance is available to both parties, then the strict liability rule and the negligence rule are both efficient. And if, somewhat more realistically, imperfect insurance is available to the injurer because of the moral hazard problem but perfect insurance is available to the victim, then the negligence rule is efficient but the strict liability rule is not. Obviously, if the simple version of the driver-pedestrian example is not descriptive of the accident situation — that is, if the injurer's activity level or the victim's care or activity level also matter — the specific conclusions in this chapter would have to be modified. However, the basic observations developed here about the interaction among liability rules, risk allocation, and insurance would carry over to other accident situations.

CHAPTER 10

SIXTH APPLICATION — LAW ENFORCEMENT USING FINES

All of the applications thus far — nuisance law, breach of contract, and automobile accidents — have been concerned with the choice of legal rules to govern disputes in which one party (the victim) brings an action against the other party (the injurer) to enforce the rule. In many areas of law, however, the victim is not relied on to do the enforcing, at least not exclusively. For example, laws controlling activities such as speeding or double parking, polluting the air, evading taxes, littering a highway, and attempting to monopolize an industry are enforced by public agencies instead of, or in addition to, private parties. Thus, to complement the discussions of the previous applications, we will now focus on the extent to which laws should be enforced, rather than on the choice of the rules themselves. The present chapter will analyze law enforcement when the sanction is a fine; the next chapter will consider the sanction of imprisonment.

The economic analysis of fines will be undertaken through an example concerned with the control of double parking. Imagine a city, called Econville, in which each of the several million residents owns a car. (Econville obviously is situated in California.) Since on-street parking often is very difficult to find in Econville, residents occasionally double park. This practice disrupts the flow of traffic and thereby imposes costs, in the form of annoyance and lost time, on other Econville drivers. The total cost imposed on other drivers is assumed to be $10 for each incident of double parking.

The benefits from double parking depend on the circumstances leading to the decision to double park. These benefits might be relatively low — below $10 — if, for example, double parking allows someone to save a couple of minutes while running into a grocery store to buy a quart of ice cream. Or these benefits might be relatively high — above $10 — if, for example, double parking saves several minutes while running into a drugstore to obtain an urgently needed medicine. It is assumed that, of the several million residents in Econville, only 100,000 individuals each year obtain benefits from double parking that exceed the $10 cost created by double parking.

As the above discussion suggests, some double-parking incidents in Econville are efficient — those in which the benefits from double parking exceed the $10 congestion cost imposed on others. All other instances of double parking are inefficient. Thus, ideally, there would be only 100,000 double-parking incidents in Econville each year, those involving residents whose benefit from double parking exceeds $10.

To attempt to achieve this result, the City Council of Econville is considering levying a fine for double parking and hiring inspectors to detect violators. The highest effective fine that can be imposed on a double-parking violator equals the wealth of that individual. It is assumed that each Econville resident has wealth of $10,000. The cost of a full-time inspector is assumed to be $100,000 per year (including the cost of her car, gas, etc.). For simplicity, it is assumed that the City Council only has three options with respect to the number of inspectors it can hire. If it hires ten inspectors at a total cost of $1 million per year, every double-parking violation will be detected. If it hires one inspector at a cost of $100,000 per year, one out of every ten violators will be caught. And if it hires one inspector on a very limited basis — one day every three months — at a cost of $1,000 per year, one out of every thousand violations will be detected. These options are summarized in the first two columns of Table 8 (ignore for now the remaining columns).

The City Council must decide both how much to spend on enforcement — choosing from among the three options — and, given the resulting probability of detection, how high to set the fine. It is assumed that the City Council is interested

TABLE 8

Fines Example — Residents Risk Neutral

Total Enforcement Costs	Probability of Detection	Fine	Expected Fine
(1)	(2)	(3)	(4)
$1,000,000	1.0	$10	$10
$500,000	.1	$100	$10
$1,000	.001	$10,000	$10

in the most efficient system of law enforcement. This means that it will want to deter inefficient double-parking violations (those in which the benefit from the violation is less than the $10 cost) but not efficient violations, and that it will want to achieve this outcome at the least possible cost.

The Risk-Neutral Case

For reasons that will become apparent, the efficient system of law enforcement depends on whether the residents of Econville are risk neutral or risk averse. Suppose that they are all neutral with respect to risk (they care only about expected outcomes). Then, in deciding whether to double park, a resident of Econville will compare his benefit from double parking to the expected fine — the fine multiplied by the probability of detection. Therefore, to achieve optimal deterrence — that is, deterrence only of those double-parking violations in which the benefits are less than the $10 congestion cost — it is necessary for the expected fine to equal $10. If the expected fine were greater than $10, some double-parking incidents in which the benefit exceeded the cost would be deterred, and if it were less than $10, some violations in which the benefit was less than the cost would nonetheless occur.

Given each possible expenditure on enforcement and the resulting probability of detection, the fine can be set so that the *expected* fine equals $10. To see this, refer again to Table 8.

If detection is certain, then the fine should be $10. If the probability of detection is .1, then a $100 fine will result in a $10 expected fine. And if the probability of detection is .001, a fine of $10,000 is necessary to generate an expected fine of $10. Thus, if the fine is set appropriately, the optimal deterrence of double-parking violations can be achieved with each expenditure on enforcement.

This observation immediately suggests what the efficient system of law enforcement is for Econville. Because optimal deterrence can be achieved with each expenditure on enforcement, there is no reason not to spend the least amount possible. In other words, the City Council should hire a part-time inspector for $1,000 per year, catch one out of every thousand double-parking violators, and fine each violator $10,000. Because the expected fine is $10, only those individuals who gain more than this amount will double park, and the City Council will have achieved this result at the least possible cost.

This example illustrates a basic principle in the economic analysis of law enforcement, which was first formalized by Gary S. Becker:[49] If individuals are risk neutral, then the efficient system of law enforcement is the one in which the fine is as large as possible — equal to the wealth of the individuals whose behavior is being controlled. This allows the probability of detection to be very low in order to save enforcement costs.[50] Note that the logic of this result does not depend on the magnitude of the costs imposed on others by the harmful activity. Thus, for example, if some activity imposed only a $1 cost on others, it still would be efficient to use as large a fine as possible — $10,000 in the example — in order to achieve optimal deterrence with the smallest possible expenditure on enforcement.

Obviously, this result is not descriptive of actual enforce-

49. Gary S. Becker, Crime and Punishment: An Economic Approach, 76 J. Pol. Econ. 169 (1968).

50. When the simplifying assumption that everyone has the same level of wealth is made more realistic, the statement of this principle becomes more complicated. However, the basic idea that the fine should be high in order to save enforcement costs still applies.

ment policies. Individuals rarely are fined an amount approximating their wealth, especially for engaging in activities that impose relatively small costs on others. Although there is nothing logically wrong with the preceding argument, it is premised on an assumption — risk neutrality — that is not likely to be correct when the fine is as high as the wealth of the individuals whose behavior is being controlled. Individuals may care only about the expected loss if the worst possible loss is small relative to their wealth, but they are likely to care as well about the actual probability and magnitude of the loss if the worst possible loss is large relative to their wealth. We therefore will reexamine the law enforcement problem when individuals are assumed to be risk averse.

The Risk-Averse Case

The residents of Econville also can be optimally deterred from double parking if they are risk averse. However, the probability of detection and/or the fine generally have to be lowered from the level derived in the risk-neutral case. This is because, given the same probability of detection and fine, a risk-averse person would be deterred more than a risk-neutral person. The risk-neutral person will double park if his benefit exceeds the expected fine. But the risk-averse person will double park only if his benefit exceeds the expected fine plus a *risk premium* that reflects his dislike of risk per se. Thus, if the probability of detection and the fine were to stay at their same levels as in the risk-neutral case, the risk-averse person would be *over*deterred. Optimal deterrence can be achieved by lowering the probability or fine appropriately — until the sum of the expected fine and the risk premium equals the harm caused. Then, a risk-averse person would double park whenever the benefit from double parking exceeds the harm caused.

For example, suppose again that the probability of detection is .1 and the fine is $100, making the expected fine $10. As seen above, a risk-neutral person would double park if the benefit from double parking exceeds the expected fine of $10. But a risk-averse person would add, say, a $1 risk premium to the expected fine and would double park only if his benefit from double parking exceeds $11. Because the cost imposed on others from double parking is only $10, there would be too few instances of double parking. This problem can be corrected by lowering the fine. For example, given a probability of detection of .1, suppose the fine is lowered to $90, making the expected fine $9. Then, assuming the risk premium is still $1, a risk-averse resident of Econville will double park if his benefit from doing so exceeds $10 — the desired outcome.[51]

The same result can be achieved when the probability of detection is .001. In the risk-neutral case, it was optimal to set the fine at $10,000 so that the expected fine was $10. But now suppose the fine has to be lowered to $2,000 to avoid overdeterring the risk-averse residents of Econville. This results in an expected fine of $2 and, it will be supposed, a risk premium of $8. (Lowering the probability of detection and raising the fine tends to increase the risk premium.) Again, a risk-averse resident of Econville will double park if his benefit from doing so exceeds $10.

Table 9 summarizes the discussion thus far of the double-parking example when individuals are risk averse. The first five columns of the table show, for each probability of detection, the fine that results in optimal deterrence, the expected fine, the risk premium, and the sum of the expected fine and the risk premium (ignore for now the remaining columns in the table). Note that, for each probability of detection, the fine is chosen so that the sum of the expected fine and the risk premium equals the $10 harm caused by double parking. Table 9 and the preceding discussion illustrate an important general point regarding optimal deterrence when individuals are risk averse: Given the probability of detection, it always is possible to set the level of the fine so that the sum of the expected fine and the risk premium equals the cost to others of an

---

51. Because the reduction of the fine discussed in the text is relatively small, it is assumed for simplicity that the risk premium remains the same. In general, however, changes in the fine or probability of detection will affect the risk premium.

TABLE 9
Fines Example — Residents Risk Averse

Probability of Detection (1)	Fine (2)	Expected Fine (3)[a]	Risk Premium (4)[b]	Expected Fine Plus Risk Premium (5)[c]	Risk-Bearing Costs (6)[c]	Enforcement Costs (7)	Risk-Bearing Costs Plus Enforcement Costs (8)
1.0	$10	$10	$0	$10	$0	$1,000,000	$1,000,000
.1	$90	$9	$1	$10	$100,000	$100,000	$200,000
.001	$2,000	$2	$8	$10	$800,000	$1,000	$801,000

a. Equals column (1) times column (2).
b. There is no risk premium in the first row because detection is certain.
c. Equals column (4) times 100,000.

individual's harmful activity.[52] The individual then will engage in the harmful activity only when his benefit from doing so exceeds the cost. Thus, it always is possible to achieve optimal deterrence, whether individuals are risk neutral or risk averse. The only difference is that, given the probability of detection, the optimal fine has to be lower for a risk-averse person than for a risk-neutral person. Otherwise, the risk-averse person would be overdeterred.

It might appear at this point that the optimal system of law enforcement when individuals are risk averse is the one in which, as in the risk-neutral case, the lowest probability of detection is chosen to save enforcement costs. It is true in the example that optimal deterrence can be achieved with the least expenditure on enforcement by using the lowest probability of detection. But this is only half of the story in the risk-averse case. The lower the probability of detection and the higher the fine, the more risk is imposed on individuals who do double park. Recall from the discussion in Chapter 7 that it is desirable to reduce or eliminate the risk borne by risk-averse persons. In the law enforcement context, this can be done by raising the probability of detection and lowering the fine accordingly. In the limit, if detection is certain, no risk is imposed on those individuals who double park. Thus, there is a conflict between minimizing the cost of enforcement and minimizing the "cost" of bearing risk. The optimal combination of the probability of detection and fine is the one that minimizes the *sum* of these costs. Before applying this principle to the double-parking example, we need to be more explicit about what is meant by the cost of bearing risk.

As seen in Chapter 7, the value of eliminating a detrimental risk can be measured by the difference between the expected value of the risk and the greatest amount of money the person

---

52. This statement is not correct if the probability of detection is very low. This is because, given a low enough probability, even a fine equal to the wealth of the individual being controlled will result in the sum of the expected fine and the risk premium being less than the cost to others of that individual's activity. This problem does not arise in the double-parking example because of the particular values chosen for the lowest probability considered and for the wealth of Econville residents.

bearing the risk would pay to avoid it.[53] In the example there, a person was willing to pay up to $130,000 to avoid a risk with an expected loss of $100,000. Thus, the value of removing the risk would be $30,000. Equivalently, if the risk is not removed, we can say that the cost of bearing the risk is $30,000. In general, the cost of bearing a risk is the difference between how much one would be willing to pay to avoid it and the expected value of the risk.

These observations now can be applied to the double-parking example. We have used the term "risk premium" in this chapter to refer to a risk-averse individual's dislike of risk per se. This is the same thing as the difference between what someone would be willing to pay to avoid a detrimental risk and the expected value of the risk. Thus, the risk premium measures the cost of bearing risk for each individual who double parks and who is subjected to the risk of being fined. Total risk-bearing costs equal the risk premium multiplied by the number of residents who double park. Given optimal deterrence, only residents whose benefits from double parking exceed the costs imposed on others will double park. It was assumed earlier in this chapter that there are 100,000 such individuals in Econville each year. Thus, for example, when the probability of detection is .1 and the fine is $90, the risk premium is $1 (see Table 9); total risk-bearing costs then are $100,000. The sixth column in Table 9 shows, for each probability of detection and fine combination, the total risk-bearing costs of the individuals who double park.

The seventh column of Table 9 reproduces the enforcement cost data from Table 8, and the last column shows the sum of the risk-bearing costs and the enforcement costs. It is clear from the last column of Table 9 that the optimal system of law enforcement in this example is to choose a probability of detection of .1 and a fine of $90. Although this choice does not minimize enforcement costs alone or risk-bearing costs alone, it does minimize their sum. Relative to this choice, using the .001 probability of detection with a $2,000 fine is inefficient because this combination increases risk-bearing

53. See pp. 59-60 above.

costs by $700,000 ($800,000 − $100,000), but reduces enforce-
ment costs only by $99,000 ($100,000 − $1,000). And raising
the probability so that detection is certain, together with a
$10 fine, is inefficient because this combination increases en-
forcement costs by $900,000 ($1,000,000 − $100,000), while
reducing risk-bearing costs only by $100,000.

The discussion of the double-parking example when the
residents are assumed to be risk averse illustrates the following
general observations. If individuals are risk averse, then the
efficient system of law enforcement is one in which the fine
generally is not as large as possible and the probability of
detection generally is not as low as it would be if individuals
were risk neutral. This is because the savings in enforcement
costs from using a low probability and a high fine must be
balanced against the increased risk imposed on those individuals for whom it is efficient to engage in the harmful activity.
Thus, the optimal probability of detection and fine depend on
how much enforcement costs decline as the probability of
detection decreases and on how risk averse the relevant individuals are. Note that if these individuals are neutral with
respect to risk, then, according to this argument, there is no
reason not to raise the fine to the wealth of the individuals
being controlled in order to lower the probability of detection.
However, as mentioned earlier, it is not plausible to assume
that individuals are risk neutral when all of their wealth is at
risk.

An important assumption in the discussion of the double-
parking example was that it is efficient for some individuals
to engage in the harmful activity. This would seem to be a
reasonable assumption in the context of double parking. But
there are other harmful activities in which the benefits from
engaging in them are never — or hardly ever — greater than
the costs they impose on others. For example, this generally
would be the case with respect to activities classified as serious
crimes, such as assault and battery or drunken driving. For
these types of activities, the optimal number of individuals
engaging in them is, let us suppose, zero. If deterrence is suc-

cessful, no one will be participating in the activity and, there-fore, no one will be bearing any risk of being fined. Thus, the optimal system of law enforcement would be the one in which the fine is as high as possible and the probability of detection is correspondingly low *even if* the individuals whose behavior is being controlled are risk averse. There will not be any risk imposed on these individuals if deterrence is successful.[54]

Obviously, in practice, deterrence is not complete and some individuals will engage in these kinds of harmful activi-ties. But the general point of this discussion is valid nonethe-less. The smaller the number of individuals whose benefits from engaging in a harmful activity exceed the costs imposed on others, the lower the optimal probability of detection and the higher the optimal fine. Although there will be risk im-posed on those individuals who do engage in the activity, the aggregate risk-bearing costs will be relatively small because there are few such individuals. It therefore is desirable to use a relatively low probability of detection and a relatively high fine in order to save enforcement costs.

Another important assumption that was implicit in the discussion of the double-parking example was that there were no mistakes in the law enforcement system. In general, if individuals are risk averse, then to the extent that there are mistakes, the probability of detection should be higher and the fine should be lower than they would be otherwise. To see why, consider the control of speeding rather than double parking, and suppose police radar equipment occasionally mal-functions and indicates that someone is speeding when he is not. Then the risk created by the probability of detection and

54. These observations can be illustrated in Table 9 with one modifica-tion. Instead of assuming that the efficient number of double-parking viola-tions is 100,000, assume that this number is zero. Column (4) still can be interpreted as the risk-bearing cost for each individual who engages in the harmful activity. But column (6), total risk-bearing costs (which equals column (4) multiplied by the efficient number of double-parking violators), would now consist of entries of zero. Thus, column (8), total risk-bearing costs plus total enforcement costs, would be the same as column (7), total enforcement costs. The optimal system of enforcement then would be to deter double parking by using a probability of detection of .001 and a fine of $10,000, even though the residents of Econville are risk averse.

the fine is imposed on many innocent drivers, not just those who speed. Hence, if mistakes are possible, the risk-bearing costs would be larger than otherwise, and the optimal system of law enforcement generally would involve a higher probability of detection and a lower fine in order to reduce these costs.

This chapter has provided an overview of the economic analysis of law enforcement when fines are used as the sanction. A central idea in this analysis, associated with the work of Gary S. Becker, is that enforcement costs can be reduced, without sacrificing optimal deterrence, by lowering the probability of detection and raising the fine accordingly. We have seen that enforcement cost considerations are of primary importance if individuals are neutral with respect to risk. These considerations also are of principal importance if individuals are averse to risk, *provided* that optimal deterrence leads to no one engaging in the harmful activity and that there are no mistakes in the enforcement system. However, if individuals are risk averse and if it is optimal for some of them to engage in the activity, or if there are mistakes, then risk-bearing considerations also are relevant. We have observed that taking these considerations into account generally increases the optimal probability of detection and decreases the optimal fine. The particular probability and fine combination that is best depends on the tradeoff between enforcement costs and risk-bearing costs.

CHAPTER 11

SEVENTH APPLICATION — LAW ENFORCEMENT USING IMPRISONMENT

In this chapter we will continue our discussion of law enforcement by considering imprisonment as the sanction rather than a fine. Imprisonment is used as a sanction in many contexts, including for most harmful acts classified as serious crimes, such as armed robbery, embezzlement, and drug dealing. While individuals who commit crimes also may be subject to fines, we will, for simplicity, focus on the case in which imprisonment is the sole sanction employed to deter such behavior.[55]

The discussion will be based on an example in which an individual steals an automobile. The state must decide how long a jail term to impose on the individual if he is caught and how much to spend on trying to catch such thieves. Obviously, a higher probability of detection will cost the state more in enforcement resources. Also, the longer the jail term, the more must be spent on operating and maintaining jails.

For reasons that will become apparent, the efficient choice of the imprisonment sentence and the probability of detection depends on how rapidly the disutility from time in jail rises with the length of the jail sentence. We will consider three cases.[56]

---

55. The use of fines and imprisonment together is considered briefly at the end of this chapter.

56. Although the examination of imprisonment in the present chapter and that of fines in the previous chapter could be undertaken using a common analytical approach, we will, for expositional simplicity, deal with

Disutility Rises Proportionally

First, suppose an individual's disutility from time in jail rises proportionally with the length of time he is in jail. For concreteness, imagine that he suffers 100 units of disutility during each year of jail time. Then, for example, a two-year sentence, resulting in 200 units of disutility, would be perceived as exactly twice as unpleasant as a one-year sentence, causing 100 units of disutility.

Suppose, to discourage the stealing of cars, the state wishes to impose 100 units of disutility on car thieves.[57] This could be accomplished by catching them for sure (assume this is possible) and putting them in jail for one year. But consider two alternatives. Suppose the state could impose a two-year sentence on the thief if he is caught, causing him to bear 200 units of disutility. If the chance of detection is .5, his expected disutility will be 100 units (.5 × 200 units of disutility), so he would be deterred to the same extent as he would be if he knows he'll go to jail for one year with certainty. Finally, suppose the state could impose a five-year sentence, corresponding to 500 units of disutility. If the probability of detection is .2, the thief's expected disutility again will be 100 units (.2 × 500 units of disutility). These options are summarized in Table 10 (ignore for now the last two columns).

Clearly, an efficient system of law enforcement will be one in which the desired level of deterrence is achieved as cheaply as possible. There are two costs to consider — the cost of enforcement and the cost of imprisonment. Suppose, as in Chapter 10, that it would cost $1 million to set the probability of detection equal to 1, and that the cost of employing a lower probability is a proportional fraction of this cost. Thus, the

---

these topics somewhat differently. (Some of these differences are discussed in footnotes below.)

57. We will not consider in this chapter how the state decides how much to deter a particular type of crime — that is, what level of disutility to impose on offenders. The factors that bear on this decision, including the harm to the victim and the gain to the offender, are similar to those discussed in Chapter 10, though an additional consideration here is the cost of imprisonment.

TABLE 10

Imprisonment Example — Disutility Rises Proportionally

Imprison-ment Sentence	Units of Disutility	Probability of Detection	Expected Disutility	Enforce-ment Costs	Imprison-ment Costs
(1)	(2)[a]	(3)	(4)[b]	(5)[c]	(6)[d]
1 year	100 units	1.0	100 units	$1,000,000	$750,000
2 years	200 units	.5	100 units	$500,000	$750,000
5 years	500 units	.2	100 units	$200,000	$750,000

a. Equals column (1) times 100 units/year.
b. Equals column (2) times column (3).
c. Equals column (3) times $1,000,000.
d. Equals 10 persons times column (3) times column (1) times $75,000/year.

cost of achieving a probability of detection of .5 would be $500,000 (.5 × $1 million), and the cost of a probability of .2 would be $200,000 (.2 × $1 million). These results are shown in the fifth column of Table 10.

The cost of imprisonment depends on the number of person-years of jail time that is served. For concreteness, assume that there are ten car thieves. If they are caught for sure and each imprisoned for one year, a total of ten person-years of jail time will be served. Suppose it costs the state $75,000 a year to keep a person in jail. Then total imprisonment costs would be $750,000 (10 person-years × $75,000 per year). Alternatively, suppose the imprisonment sentence is two years and the probability of detection is .5. Then five of the ten car thieves would be caught,[58] with each serving two years, so the total number of person-years would again be ten. Consequently, total imprisonment costs also would be $750,000. Finally, if the jail sentence is five years and the probability of detection is .2, two car thieves will be caught and they will serve a total of ten person-years of jail time, again costing the state $750,000. These results are shown in the sixth column

58. The actual number of thieves who would be caught is uncertain, but five represents the expected value of the number who will be caught.

of Table 10. Notably, in the present case, the cost of imprisonment is the same under all three combinations of the probability of detection and the sentence.[59]

This discussion demonstrates that if the disutility from imprisonment is proportional to the length of time in jail, the efficient system of law enforcement involves using relatively high sentences and correspondingly low probabilities of detection. This is because, as the sentence is raised and the probability of detection is lowered proportionally so as to maintain deterrence, the total cost of imprisonment is unaffected, but the cost of detection declines significantly.

Disutility Rises More than Proportionally

Now suppose an individual's disutility from imprisonment rises more than proportionally with the length of time he is in jail. This form of disutility would describe a person for whom prison becomes increasingly difficult to tolerate as time passes, or for whom separation from family, friends, and everyday life becomes more and more painful. For concreteness, imagine that such an individual suffers 100 units of disutility during the first year in jail, 200 units during the second year, 300 units during the third year, and so forth. Then, for example, a two-year sentence, imposing 300 units of disutility (100 units + 200 units), would be perceived as three times as unpleasant as a one-year sentence, causing 100 units of disutility.

Assume again that the state wishes to inflict 100 units of disutility on car thieves. This could be accomplished by catching offenders with certainty and putting them in jail for one year. Alternatively, suppose the state imposes a two-year sentence on the offender if he is caught, causing him to bear 300 units of disutility (100 units + 200 units). If the chance

59. Another cost of imprisonment, besides the cost of jails, is the disutility borne by prisoners. This cost can be ignored here because it will be held constant throughout the analysis (see the fourth columns of Tables 10, 11, and 12).

TABLE 11

Imprisonment Example — Disutility Rises More than Proportionally

Imprisonment Sentence	Disutility	Probability of Detection	Expected Disutility	Enforce- ment Costs	Imprison- ment Costs
(1)	(2)[a]	(3)	(4)[b]	(5)[c]	(6)[d]
1 year	100 units	1.0	100 units	$1,000,000	$750,000
2 years	300 units	.333	100 units	$333,333	$500,000
5 years	1,500 units	.067	100 units	$66,667	$250,000

a. See discussion in text.
b. Equals column (2) times column (3).
c. Equals column (3) times $1,000,000.
d. Equals 10 persons times column (3) times column (1) times $75,000/year.

of detection is .333, his expected disutility will be 100 units (.333 × 300 units of disutility),[60] so he would be deterred to the same extent as he would be if he knows he'll go to jail for sure for one year. Finally, suppose the state imposes a five-year sentence, corresponding to 1,500 units of disutility (100 units + 200 units + 300 units + 400 units + 500 units). If the chance of detection is .067, the offender's expected disutility again will be 100 units (.067 × 1,500 units of disutility). These options are summarized in Table 11 (ignore for now the last two columns).

The cost of enforcement still is assumed to be $1 million if the probability of detection is 1, and scaled down proportionally if the probability is less than 1. Thus, if a probability of detection of .333 is employed, enforcement costs would be $333,333 (.333 × $1 million), and if a probability of .067 is used, enforcement costs would be $66,667 (.067 × $1 million). These results are shown in the fifth column of Table 11.

60. For simplicity, probabilities are stated in the text with no more than three significant digits. When performing calculations using these probabilities, however, a greater number of significant digits is used. Relying on the probabilities in the text may lead to superficial discrepancies, as here (where multiplying 300 units of disutility by .333 results in 99.9 units of disutility, not 100 units).

As previously, assume that the cost of imprisoning one person for a year is $75,000 and that there are ten car thieves, so if they are caught for sure and imprisoned for one year, total imprisonment costs would be $750,000 (10 person-years × $75,000 per year). Alternatively, if they are caught with a probability of .333 and the imprisonment sentence is two years, total imprisonment costs would be $500,000 (.333 × 10 persons × 2 years × $75,000 per year). Finally, if they are caught with a probability of .067 and the imprisonment sentence is five years, total imprisonment costs would be $250,000 (.067 × 10 persons × 5 years × $75,000 per year). These results are shown in the sixth column of Table 11.

It is clear from this discussion that if the disutility from imprisonment rises more than proportionally with the length of time in jail, the efficient system of law enforcement again involves using high sentences and low probabilities of detection. As in the previous case, if the sentence is raised and the probability of detection is lowered so as to maintain deterrence, the cost of detection declines significantly. Note that this benefit — lower enforcement costs — is even greater than in the case in which the disutility from jail time rises proportionally. In that case, the probability of detection could be lowered proportionally without sacrificing deterrence, whereas here the probability can be lowered more than proportionally (because the disutility from jail time is rising more than proportionally).

Additionally, as the sentence is raised and the probability of detection is lowered, with deterrence constant, the cost of imprisonment declines significantly. This is because the expected value of the prison term declines. Specifically, if the sentence is one year and the probability of detection is 1, then, obviously, the "expected" sentence is one year. If the sentence is two years and the probability of detection is .333, however, the expected sentence declines to .667 years (.333 × 2 years). And if the sentence is five years and the probability of detection is .067, the expected sentence is only .333 years (.067 × 5 years). This reason for raising the sentence and lowering the probability of detection was not applicable when the disutility of imprisonment rose proportionally with the length of time in jail (there the expected sentence remained constant at one year), but provides a further rationale in the present case for employing a relatively high sentence and a correspondingly low probability of detection. This added benefit is due to the fact that the potency of the sentence rises more than in proportion to its length, so that, in essence, shorter average sentences can be used.

Disutility Rises Less than Proportionally

Finally, suppose an individual's disutility from time in jail rises less than proportionally with the sentence. This might be because a person becomes accustomed to prison life or because he ceases to care as much about those he knew from the outside. Also, the disutility associated with the first year of prison might be particularly great compared to that of later years for the following reasons: humiliation of the prisoner may occur early on and do its major harm then; and stigmatization of the prisoner (which lowers earning capacity and status) may result after spending even a modest length of time in jail, and not increase much with the number of years spent there.[61]

For concreteness, imagine that an individual suffers 100 units of disutility during the first year in jail, and then half as much each successive year as the year before. Thus, the individual would bear 50 units of disutility during the second year, 25 units during the third year, and so forth. A two-year sentence, causing 150 units of disutility (100 units + 50 units), would be perceived as one-and-a-half times as unpleasant as a one-year sentence, which would cause 100 units of disutility.

To make car thieves bear 100 units of disutility, the state could catch them for sure and put them in jail for one year. Alternatively, a two-year sentence, causing 150 units of disutility, combined with a chance of detection of .667, would result in expected disutility of 100 units (.667 × 150 units of

---

61. A related phenomenon is that individuals may "discount" jail time served in the future, just as they treat a financial obligation due in the future as less burdensome than the same obligation due immediately.

TABLE 12

Imprisonment Example — Disutility Rises Less than Proportionally

Imprison- ment Sentence	Disutility	Proba- bility of Detection	Expected Disutility	Enforce- ment Costs	Imprison- ment Costs	Sum of Costs
(1)	(2)ᵃ	(3)	(4)ᵇ	(5)ᶜ	(6)ᵈ	(7)ᵉ
1 year	100 units	1.0	100 units	$1,000,000	$750,000	$1,750,000
2 years	150 units	.667	100 units	$666,667	$1,000,000	$1,666,667
5 years	194 units	.516	100 units	$516,129	$1,935,484	$2,451,613

a. See discussion in text.
b. Equals column (2) times column (3).
c. Equals column (3) times $1,000,000.
d. Equals 10 persons times column (3) times column (1) times $75,000/year.
e. Equals sum of column (5) and column (6).

disutility). Finally, if the state imposes a five-year sentence, approximately 194 units of disutility (100 units + 50 units + 25 units + 12.5 units + 6.25 units) will be borne by the offender; if the chance of detection is .516, his expected disutility also will be 100 units (.516 × 194 units of disutility). These options are summarized in Table 12 (ignore for now the last three columns).

As in the previous cases, the cost of enforcement declines as the probability of detection is lowered. Specifically, enforcement costs are $1,000,000 if the probability of detection is 1, $666,667 if the probability of detection is .667 (.667 × $1,000,000), and $516,129 if the probability of detection is .516 (.516 × $1,000,000). These results are shown in the fifth column of Table 12.

Unlike in the previous cases, however, the cost of imprisonment increases if the sentence is raised and the probability of detection is lowered in a way that keeps deterrence constant. Imprisonment costs are $750,000 if offenders are caught for sure and imprisoned for one year (10 person-years × $75,000 per year), $1,000,000 if they are caught with a probability of .667 and imprisoned for two years (.667 × 10 persons × 2 years × $75,000 per year), and $1,935,484 if they are caught with a probability of .516 and imprisoned for five years (.516 × 10 persons × 5 years × $75,000 per year). These results are shown in the sixth column of Table 12.

Why does the cost of imprisonment rise in the present case, but not in the earlier cases? The reason is that, now if the sentence is raised, the disutility from imprisonment increases relatively little. As a result, the probability of detection cannot be lowered very much — less than proportionally — if deterrence is to be maintained. To illustrate this point in the extreme, suppose the disutility from a ten-year sentence were negligibly greater than the disutility from a five-year sentence. Then the probability of detection could be lowered only very slightly if the sentence is raised from five years to ten years. The expected value of the sentence would approximately double, and so would imprisonment costs.

This illustration essentially explains the outcome in the present case. Raising the sentence from two years to five years — more than doubling the sentence — only raises the disutility associated with imprisonment from 150 units to 194 units. Consequently, the probability of detection cannot decline much, from .667 to .516, if deterrence is to be maintained. The two-year sentence with a probability of detection of .667 has an expected sentence of 1.33 years (.667 × 2 years), while the five-year sentence with a probability of detection of .516 has an expected sentence of 2.58 years (.516 × 5 years). The expected sentence nearly doubled, causing imprisonment costs to nearly double (see the sixth column of Table 12).

In the present case, therefore, raising the imprisonment sentence and lowering the probability of detection, while keeping deterrence constant, has conflicting effects on the cost of enforcement and the cost of imprisonment. The former cost declines but the latter rises. The optimal choice of the sentence and the probability of detection depends on the relative strength of these two effects. The combination of the sentence and the probability that minimizes the sum of enforcement costs and imprisonment costs will be the most efficient one. In the present example, this sum is $1,750,000 if the sentence is one year and the probability of detection is 1 ($1,000,000 + $750,000), $1,666,667 if the sentence is two years and the probability is .667 ($666,667 + $1,000,000), and $2,451,613 if the sentence is five years and the probability is .516 ($516,129 + $1,935,484). These results are provided in the seventh column of Table 12. Hence, in this example, the optimal sentence is two years and the optimal probability of detection is .667.

The discussion in this chapter shows that a general advantage of relying on relatively high imprisonment sentences is that the probability of detection needed to accomplish the desired level of deterrence can be lowered. This point is analogous to one made in Chapter 10 with respect to monetary sanctions. However, if the disutility of imprisonment rises less than proportionally with the length of the sentence, which seems quite plausible for the reasons discussed above, raising the sentence and lowering the probability of detection so as to maintain deterrence implies that the cost of imprisonment will rise. Hence, in this case, the enforcement cost savings may well be offset by the imprisonment cost increase, making a relatively short imprisonment sentence, combined with a correspondingly higher probability of detection, more desirable. The analysis in this case may therefore provide one reason why imprisonment sentences are not uniformly high in practice.[62]

In conclusion, two important observations regarding imprisonment sanctions are worth noting. First, although this chapter has, for simplicity, considered imprisonment sanctions without also considering fines, imprisonment sentences should not be employed without first exhausting the use of monetary sanctions. The reason is simple: fines are a less expensive sanction for society to impose than are imprison-

62. The three cases discussed in this chapter could be said to describe individuals who are, respectively, risk neutral, risk averse, and risk preferring with respect to time in jail. Differences between the analysis of imprisonment in these cases and the corresponding analysis of fines are due to the fact that imprisonment is a more costly sanction than is a fine (see the next paragraph in the text).

ment sentences. Fines are essentially transfers of money from the offender to the government, whereas imprisonment sentences require the government to spend money to build and maintain jails (plus the offender's productivity is lost). Consequently, imprisonment sanctions should not be relied upon unless the offender also is fined to the maximum extent feasible.

The second observation concerns the rationale for using imprisonment sanctions. Our analysis considered how the prospect of bearing an imprisonment sentence, like the prospect of bearing a fine, can deter unwanted conduct. But another rationale for using imprisonment sentences is to "incapacitate" potential offenders — to prevent them from causing harm even if they can't be deterred from doing so. The economic analysis of this rationale for imprisonment is beyond the scope of our discussion, but it is potentially a very important reason for employing imprisonment sanctions.

CHAPTER 12
COMPETITIVE MARKETS

In the nuisance law and breach of contract applications, it was assumed that at least one of the parties to the dispute was a firm rather than an individual. Examples of other kinds of disputes in which firms frequently are involved include those related to widespread pollution or defective products. These are the next two applications that will be discussed. Before addressing them, it will be useful to describe certain features of competitive markets.

A *competitive market* is a market in which there are many firms producing the same commodity and many consumers purchasing it. In such a market, each producer believes that he has no control over the prevailing price of the commodity because he supplies such a small fraction of it. Similarly, each consumer believes that he has no control over the price because he buys such a small fraction of the total amount sold.[63] Our discussion of competitive markets will assume that firms presently in the industry are free to leave the industry if profit opportunities are better elsewhere, and that new firms are free to enter this industry if it is more profitable than alternative investment opportunities. This assumption of free exit and

63. More generally, one could characterize markets in terms of the degree to which each seller or buyer has control over the market price. A competitive market is one important special case. A monopolistic market, in which there is a single seller who sets the price, and many buyers, is another. Although the next two applications — pollution control and products liability — could be considered in the context of markets that are not competitive, it is beyond the scope of this book to undertake this task. The style of analysis would be similar to that used in the competitive case (although the specific conclusions would differ).

free entry of firms defines what economists refer to as the *long run*.[64] When all firms that want to leave the industry have done so and when all firms that want to enter have done so, the industry is said to be in *long-run equilibrium*.

Price Equals Cost

A basic principle of competitive markets in long-run equilibrium is that the price of a product will equal its cost of production.[65] Why this must be so can easily be explained by an example. Suppose it costs $100 to manufacture a lawnmower. If the price of lawnmowers were below $100, say $75, then a producer would lose $25 for every lawnmower made. It would be more profitable for the firm to go out of business — that is, to exit — and to earn nothing than to lose money producing lawnmowers. Thus, in equilibrium — after all firms that want to exit have done so — the price of lawnmowers would have to be at least $100. But if the price of lawnmowers were above $100, say $150, then lawnmower production would be very profitable. New firms would enter this industry because of its profitability. Consequently, the supply of lawnmowers would increase, a glut would occur, and the price would begin to fall. As long as the price exceeds the cost of production, firms would continue to enter this industry and the price would continue to fall. Thus, in equilibrium, the price of lawnmowers would not exceed $100. This discussion shows that, because firms are free to exit and to enter the industry, the price of a product will equal its cost of production.

If the price of a product equals its cost of production, a firm producing it will just break even — obtain revenue exactly equal to its costs. This does not mean, however, that the managers of the firm will not receive any compensation or

64. In the *short run*, it is assumed that existing firms can exit but no new firms can enter.

65. Readers who previously have studied economics will recall that in a competitive long-run equilibrium, a firm's average cost equals its marginal cost. Thus, there is no ambiguity in the text in referring simply to the "cost of production."

that the owners of the firm will not earn any return on their investment in the firm. The managers' compensation and the owners' returns already are included as part of the cost of production.

The Efficiency of Competitive Pricing

Is the fact that the competitive price equals production costs desirable? This question is answered in the affirmative by another basic principle of competitive markets. This principle states that if firms take "all relevant costs" into account in setting their price, a competitive market will lead to the efficient outcome. What is meant by "all relevant costs" will become clear in the next two applications; for now, just interpret this phrase as referring to the cost of production.

To understand why the second principle is true, consider the lawnmower example again. People value lawnmowers differently. For example, someone with a large yard would be willing to pay more for a lawnmower than someone with a small yard. Assume, as before, that lawnmowers cost $100 to produce. Suppose, however, that lawnmowers sell for $150. Then someone who values a lawnmower at $125 will not buy one. But this is inefficient because the benefit of the lawnmower, $125, exceeds its production cost, $100. There would be an efficiency gain of $25 if this person were to obtain a lawnmower. Alternatively, suppose that lawnmowers are priced at $75. Then someone who values a lawnmower at $85 will purchase one. But this is inefficient too, because the benefit of the lawnmower is less than its production cost of $100. There will be an efficiency loss of $15 when this person buys a lawnmower.

In general, if a good is priced above its cost of production, then some individuals who value the good more than its cost will not buy it, which is an inefficient outcome; and if a good is priced below its production cost, then some individuals who value it less than its cost will buy it nonetheless, which also is an inefficient outcome. Only if the price of the good equals its cost of production will those people who value it more than its cost buy it and those who value it less not buy it. This is required to achieve the efficient outcome. Because, according to the first basic principle, the price of a good in a competitive market equals its cost of production, a competitive market will lead to the efficient outcome.

We will now consider two applications — pollution control and products liability — that make use of these observations about competitive markets.

CHAPTER 13

EIGHTH APPLICATION —
POLLUTION CONTROL

In this chapter we will investigate the efficiency of different legal rules for controlling pollution when the polluters are firms in a competitive industry in long-run equilibrium. The discussion will be based on an example in which firms emitting air pollution harm households downwind of the pollution. For simplicity, it is assumed that the victims of the pollution are not also consumers of the product manufactured by the firms. In the example, the harm to the victims depends on whether the firms filter their smoke before discharging it into the atmosphere. The filtering process reduces the level of pollution but does not eliminate it entirely. It also increases the polluters' cost of production. The victims of the pollution are assumed to be unable to affect the damage they suffer. (This assumption will be reconsidered below.)

The data for this example are described in Table 13 for a representative firm (ignore for now the last three columns). If the firm does not filter the pollution, its production cost per unit of output is $100 and the victims' damage per unit of output is $40. If the firm does filter the pollution, its cost per unit is $115 and the victims' damage per unit is $10. Note that, once the filtering decision has been made, there is no uncertainty with respect to the harm; thus, the issue of risk allocation does not arise in this example.

Given the data in Table 13, it is clear that the efficient solution involves filtering the pollution before discharging it. Although filtering increases production cost by $15 for each unit of the firm's output, it reduces pollution damage by $30

TABLE 13

Pollution Control Example

Behavior of Firm	Firm's Production Cost Per Unit	Victims' Pollution Damage Per Unit	Full Cost Per Unit	Firm's Cost Per Unit under Negligence	Firm's Cost Per Unit under Strict Liability
	(1)	(2)	(3)	(4)	(5)
Don't filter	$100	$40	$140	$140	$140
Filter	$115	$10	$125	$115	$125

for each unit produced. Another way to see that filtering is efficient is to note that the *full cost* of the product — the firm's production cost plus the victims' pollution damage — is $140 if filtering does not occur but only $125 if it does occur. These full cost numbers are shown in the third column of Table 13.

There is a second aspect of the efficient solution in the pollution control example. Even if filtering occurs for each unit of the good that is produced, an inefficient amount of the good may be produced. Equivalently, because goods are produced to satisfy the demands of consumers, an inefficient amount of the good may be consumed. For reasons seen in the previous chapter, an inefficient amount will be consumed either if some individuals who buy the good value it less than its full cost or if some individuals who do not buy the good value it more that its full cost. Because the full cost of the good is $125 — assuming that filtering occurs — only individuals who value the good at $125 or more per unit should consume it.

Only Polluters Determine Harm

We will now examine whether the liability rules of negligence and strict liability lead to the efficient control of pollution. Under negligence, suppose firms are liable only if they do not filter. Then, if a firm does not filter, its cost per unit totals $140 — the production cost of $100 plus a liability cost of $40 (equal to the victims' pollution damage per unit). If the firm does filter, its cost is $115 — just the production cost because it is not liable. These numbers are shown in the fourth column in Table 13. Clearly, each firm will choose to filter. Thus, in long-run equilibrium, the price will be $115 per unit. If the price were higher, entry would occur due to the profit opportunities, and if the price were lower, firms would leave the industry because they would be losing money. But if the equilibrium price is $115, excessive consumption of the good will occur. Given that firms filter, the full cost of the good is $125, including the $10 residual pollution damage borne by victims (see Table 13). Thus, at a price of $115, there will be persons who value the good at less than its full cost — for example, at $120 — but who will buy it nonetheless.

This example illustrates a general point about the effects of a negligence rule in a competitive market: Even though the rule of negligence can, with an appropriate standard of care, induce firms to take the efficient amount of care, it generally leads to an inefficient level of output because the market price does not completely reflect the full cost of the product. Specifically, the price does not include the residual damages that occur even when each firm is taking an efficient amount of care. Consequently, too much of the good will be consumed.[66]

Now consider the rule of strict liability, under which firms will be made liable for the victims' pollution damages whether they filter or not. Then, as shown in the last column of Table 13, each firm's cost, including its liability payments, would be $140 per unit if it does not filter and $125 if it does. Each firm therefore will choose to filter. Thus, in long-run equilibrium, the price of the good will be $125 and, because the full cost also is $125, the amount of the good bought by consumers will be efficient.

This example illustrates a general observation about strict

66. This problem would not arise if, when the efficient amount of care is taken, *all* pollution is eliminated. In general, however, some residual damage will occur.

liability in competitive markets: Strict liability can induce firms to take the efficient amount of care and can induce consumers to purchase the efficient amount of the product. The latter effect occurs because the market price reflects the full cost of the product, including the damages that remain even when each firm is taking the efficient amount of care.

Victims Also Affect Harm

In many pollution situations, the victims of the pollution also can affect their damages from pollution. For example, they might be able to paint their homes with more expensive pollution-resistant paint or move to a less polluted neighborhood. The conclusions in this chapter regarding the rules of negligence and strict liability would have to be modified somewhat if both the polluters' behavior and the victims' behavior can affect the level of damages. Because the analysis of this problem closely parallels the corresponding analysis of automobile accidents in Chapter 6 (when both the driver and the pedestrian can affect the pedestrian's expected accident costs),[67] the discussion here will be brief.

Suppose for concreteness that the efficient solution now requires not only that the firms filter their pollution but also that the victims paint their homes with special paint. This paint reduces the victims' damages, but it does not eliminate the damages. The efficient solution still requires that only those consumers who value the good more than its full cost purchase it. Note, however, that the appropriate full cost now equals the polluters' cost of production plus the residual damages that occur when the polluter is filtering *and* when the victims are using the special paint.

Under the rule of negligence, a polluter will choose to filter in order to avoid the liability costs that he otherwise would incur. Given this decision, the victims will bear their own losses and therefore will have an appropriate incentive to use the pollution-resistant paint. Thus, as in the automobile

67. See pp. 47-50 above.

accident example, the negligence rule can induce both the injurer and the victim to take appropriate care. However, the negligence rule still will fail to induce efficient decisions by consumers because the price of the good will not reflect the damages that occur even when the polluters and the victims are taking appropriate care.

Under strict liability, polluters also will choose to filter, as before. However, pollution victims will not have any incentive to use pollution-resistant paint because they will be fully compensated for their damages. Thus, for reasons discussed in Chapter 6 in the context of the automobile accident example, it is necessary to add a defense of contributory negligence to induce the pollution victims to take appropriate care. With this defense, the rule of strict liability will be efficient with respect to both parties' care. Because the victims will choose not to be contributorily negligent, the polluters will be liable for the victims' residual damages. Thus, the price of the product will reflect these damages and an efficient amount will be purchased.

This discussion shows that the basic conclusions about strict liability and negligence in the pollution control example are not affected if the victims can reduce their damages by taking precautions. The problem under the negligence rule is that the price of the good produced by the polluters does not reflect the damages that still occur after all of the parties have taken appropriate care. This inefficiency is corrected under the strict liability rule because the polluter is made liable for these residual damages. It is necessary, however, to add a defense of contributory negligence to the strict liability rule to create incentives for the victims to take appropriate precautions.

The conclusions in this chapter are similar to those derived in Chapter 6 in the context of automobile accidents. This should not be surprising because the basic problems that liability rules have to solve in the two contexts also are similar. In both chapters, the rules of negligence and strict liability with a defense of contributory negligence were found to be equally effective in controlling both the injurer's care (the polluter's filtering decision here, the driver's speed in Chapter 6) and the victim's care (the homeowner's painting decision here, the pedestrian's decision whether to walk or run in Chapter 6). Also, in both chapters, strict liability was found to be superior to negligence in controlling the injurer's activity level (which corresponds to the output of the industry here, the amount of driving in Chapter 6).[68] A slight difference between the two chapters is that we have not considered the activity-level issue with respect to the victim in the pollution control context. This is why strict liability with a defense of contributory negligence was found to be efficient here but was found to induce excessive participation in the activity by the pedestrian in Chapter 6.[69] In practice, however, there also might be an activity-level issue with respect to pollution victims. For example, suppose a victim's damage depends not only on whether he uses pollution-resistant paint but also on the size of the house he buys. Then the conclusions in this chapter would exactly parallel those in Chapter 6.

68. For the reasons discussed in Chapter 6, this statement presumes that the standard of care under the negligence rule is not defined in terms of the injurer's activity level. See p. 53 above.

69. See p. 54 above. Recall that this conclusion presumes that the standard of care applicable to the victim does not include the victim's activity level.

CHAPTER 14

NINTH APPLICATION — PRODUCTS LIABILITY

We will now use several of the principles developed in the chapters on competitive markets and on risk bearing and insurance to evaluate the efficiency of alternative liability rules for dealing with product accidents. The analysis will be based on an example in which a soda manufacturer must decide whether to use bottles or cans. Bottles are cheaper to produce but have higher expected accident losses.[70] It will be assumed that the victim of the accident is the purchaser of the soda and that, for simplicity, she cannot affect expected accident losses by taking care. (The possibilities that the victim is a "third party" — such as a bystander — and that the victim can reduce expected losses by taking care will be considered at the end of the chapter.)

The data for the example are provided in Table 14 (ignore for now the last column). If soda is manufactured in bottles, the production cost per unit is $1.00, the chance of an accident is 1/100,000, and the loss if an accident occurs is $10,000. The *expected* accident loss per unit therefore is 10 cents (1/100,000 × $10,000). Similarly, if soda is manufactured in cans, the production cost is $1.03, the accident probability is 1/200,000, the loss is $4,000, and the expected accident loss is 2 cents (1/200,000 × $4,000).

Given this information, it is clear that the efficient solution involves selling soda in cans. Although using cans in-

70. These losses are assumed to have a monetary value. But see note 23 above.

TABLE 14

Products Liability Example

Behavior of Firm	Firm's Cost of Production Per Unit	Probability of Accident to Consumer	Loss if Accident	Expected Accident Loss	Full Cost Per Unit
	(1)	(2)	(3)	(4)	(5)
Use bottle	$1.00	1/100,000	$10,000	10 cents	$1.10
Use can	$1.03	1/200,000	$4,000	2 cents	$1.05

creases production costs by 3 cents per unit, it lowers expected accident losses by 8 cents. Equivalently, the full cost of the product — the firm's production cost plus the consumer's expected accident loss — is less with cans ($1.05) than with bottles ($1.10). This is shown in the last column of Table 14. Another aspect of the efficient solution involves the purchasers' consumption decisions. Assuming cans are used, the full cost of soda is $1.05; therefore, only individuals who value soda at $1.05 or more should drink it. The final aspect of the efficient solution concerns the allocation of risk. Initially, however, this consideration will be put aside by assuming that producers and consumers are risk neutral.

Consumers Have Perfect Information

It will be useful to begin by comparing product liability rules when consumers are assumed to have perfect information about expected accident losses. We will consider the rules of strict liability, negligence, and no liability. Under strict liability, firms are liable to consumers for their losses whenever an accident occurs. Then, given the data in Table 14, each firm's cost per unit — including expected liability payments — would be $1.10 if bottles are used and $1.05 if cans are used. Thus, in long-run equilibrium, the price per bottle would be $1.10 and the price per can would be $1.05. Consumers clearly will prefer to purchase soda in cans.[71] Moreover, given the price of soda in cans, they will purchase an efficient number of cans because the price reflects the full cost of the product. Strict liability therefore is efficient both with respect to the care exercised by each firm — in the example, whether cans or bottles are used — and with respect to the output of the industry.

Under negligence, suppose firms are liable only if they produce soda in bottles. Then, referring to Table 14, a firm's cost would be $1.10 if bottles are used ($1.00 in production cost plus 10 cents in expected liability cost) and $1.03 if cans are used (just the production cost). Soda therefore will sell for $1.10 in bottles and for $1.03 in cans. Because consumers are assumed to have correct information about expected accident losses, they will in effect add 2 cents to the price of cans because they bear their own losses when cans are used. Consumers still will prefer cans to bottles. Although soda in cans will sell for $1.03, consumers will buy the correct amount because the *effective price,* including the additional 2 cents in expected accident costs, is $1.05. Thus, negligence also is efficient both with respect to care and output.

Under no liability, consumers bear their own losses regardless of firms' behavior. Thus, a firm's cost, and the price, would be $1.00 if bottles are used and $1.03 if cans are used. Because consumers will in effect add 10 cents to the price of bottles but only 2 cents to the price of cans, consumers only will want to buy soda in cans. And because they will treat the effective price of soda in cans as $1.05, they will purchase the correct amount. Thus, no liability also is efficient with respect to care and output.

This discussion illustrates a general result in the economic analysis of product liability rules: When producers and consumers are risk neutral and consumers have perfect information about product risks, the choice of a liability rule is

71. Consumers are assumed to enjoy drinking soda just as much out of a can as out of a bottle.

irrelevant. Every rule will be efficient in terms of the care exercised by producers and the output of the industry.[72]

Consumers Underestimate Product Risks

It is unrealistic in many product markets to assume that consumers have perfect information about expected accident losses. This assumption seems especially inappropriate for products that cause harm very infrequently. We therefore will examine the effects of imperfect consumer information on the optimal choice of a product liability rule. To see these effects in the simplest way possible, it will be assumed that consumers completely underestimate the risks — that is, they think the product is perfectly safe.

The earlier discussion of strict liability is not affected by imperfect consumer information about product risks. Given their production and liability costs, producers still would be willing to offer bottles at a price of $1.10 or cans at a price of $1.05. Consumers still only will purchase soda in cans and will, given the price, buy the correct amount. The efficiency of strict liability does not depend on the information of consumers for the following reason. Because consumers know that they will be fully compensated for product accident losses, they will treat the good as if it were perfectly safe, *regardless of their information about the product risks.* But, because firms are liable for the actual losses, consumers will be forced to take the actual risks into account through the prices charged by firms.

Under negligence, firms would be willing, as before, to sell soda in bottles for $1.10, given that they will be liable for the losses that occur, or in cans for $1.03, given that they will not be liable. Now, however, consumers will not add 2 cents to the price of cans to account for expected accident losses

---

72. This result can be viewed as an application of the simple version of the Coase Theorem: If there are zero transaction costs, the efficient outcome will occur regardless of which legal rule is chosen. See p. 14 above. The assumption here that consumers have perfect information is analogous to the assumption of zero transaction costs.

(because they are assumed to be ignorant of the product risks). They still will purchase soda in cans because soda is less expensive in cans. However, too much soda will be purchased because consumers will ignore the expected accident losses. For example, someone who values soda at $1.04 will buy a can for $1.03 even though the full cost is $1.05. The important point about negligence when consumers underestimate product risks is that, while producers still can be induced to take appropriate care, consumers will buy too much of the good because they will not fully take into account the accident losses that remain.

Under no liability, firms would be willing, as before, to offer bottles at a price of $1.00 or cans at a price of $1.03. Now, however, consumers will not add 10 cents to the price of bottles or 2 cents to the price of cans to reflect expected accident losses. As a result, consumers will purchase soda in bottles and, because they do not take into account expected accident losses, will buy too much soda. Thus, when consumers underestimate expected accident losses, the rule of no liability leads both to too little care and to excessive output.

The discussion thus far illustrates the following proposition: When consumers underestimate product risks, only the rule of strict liability is efficient both with respect to the care exercised by firms and the purchase decisions of consumers. The rule of negligence can induce producers to take appropriate care, but consumers will purchase too much of the good. And the rule of no liability is deficient both with respect to care and with respect to output. Thus, strict liability is, in effect, a substitute for perfect consumer information.[73]

Risk Aversion

It was assumed initially that both producers and consumers are risk neutral. This may be a reasonable assumption in

73. If consumers *overestimate* product risks, then producers would have an incentive to voluntarily provide full product warranties. These warranties would lead to the same outcome as the rule of strict liability.

some product liability situations, such as when the product defect leads to the destruction of the product itself but does not cause additional damage to persons or property. In other situations, however, the assumption of risk neutrality would be unrealistic, especially if there is substantial additional damage. This would be the case, for example, with respect to exploding soda bottles.

We therefore will reconsider product liability rules assuming that producers and/or consumers are risk averse. Under strict liability, product risks are borne entirely by the producers, whereas under negligence, the losses are left entirely on consumers (assuming that producers meet the standard of care). Under no liability, of course, the risks also are borne entirely by consumers. Because negligence is equivalent to no liability in terms of risk allocation, but is preferred to no liability in terms of getting producers to take care, the rule of no liability will not be considered further.

Once risk aversion is taken into account, the availability of insurance also becomes an important consideration. Because the analysis of the interaction between product liability rules and insurance closely parallels the corresponding analysis in Chapter 9 in the context of automobile accidents[74] the discussion here will be relatively brief and will focus on risk allocation issues. (The reader should keep in mind, however, that the choice of a product liability rule also will affect the care exercised by the parties and the output of the industry.)

If insurance is not available to either party, then, with respect to the allocation of risk, strict liability is ideal if consumers are risk averse and producers are risk neutral, whereas negligence is ideal if the reverse is true. If both producers and consumers are risk averse, a modified version of strict liability should be used, with the level of liability depending on the relative aversion to risk of producers and consumers. The more risk averse consumers are relative to producers, the higher should be the level of liability.

If ideal liability insurance and first-party accident insurance policies are available, then both strict liability and negli-

74. See pp. 71-78 above.

gence are efficient in terms of risk allocation. Under strict liability, producers will be fully insured by liability insurance, and under negligence, consumers will be fully insured by first-party accident insurance.

Finally, suppose that insurance policies provide less than complete coverage because of the problem of moral hazard. Under strict liability, producers would bear some risk because, given the moral hazard problem with respect to their care, liability insurance policies would be incomplete. Similarly, under negligence, consumers would bear some risk because, for reasons to be explained, there is a moral hazard problem with respect to their behavior and first-party accident insurance policies therefore would be incomplete.

Although it has been assumed that consumers cannot affect their expected accident losses by taking care, they generally *can* reduce their expected accident losses by purchasing fewer units of the good. To avoid a moral hazard problem with respect to their consumption decision, the premium for first-party accident insurance must be based on the amount purchased. For example, because the expected accident loss from drinking soda in cans rises proportionally with the number of cans purchased, the insurance premium also would have to rise proportionally with the quantity purchased. If the premium does not depend on the number of cans purchased, then consumers will buy too much soda. In general, it obviously is difficult, if not impossible, for insurance companies to monitor consumers' purchases. This certainly would be the case, for example, with respect to soda consumption. Consequently, first-party accident insurance policies would provide less than full coverage in order to discourage consumers from purchasing an excessive amount of the good.

With both imperfect liability insurance and imperfect first-party accident insurance, the optimal choice between strict liability and negligence in terms of risk allocation depends on the relative aversion to risk of producers and consumers. Under strict liability, producers will bear some risk because of incomplete liability insurance coverage, but consumers will be insured by the liability payment. Under negligence, producers will be free of liability (assuming they meet the standard of care), but consumers will bear some risk because of incomplete first-party accident insurance coverage. Thus, to the extent that consumers are more risk averse than producers, strict liability would be preferred to negligence, and vice versa.[75]

The moral hazard problem with respect to the consumer's purchase decision, leading to overconsumption, may not arise in some circumstances. For many products — such as washing machines, lawnmowers, and toaster ovens — it is reasonable to assume that each consumer needs only one unit of the good. Even if a first-party accident insurer can't monitor an individual's purchase of these goods, they are not likely to be consumed in excessive quantity by an insured. Consequently, first-party accident insurance policies would provide full coverage (still assuming that the consumer cannot affect his expected accident loss by taking care). Negligence then would be superior to strict liability in terms of risk allocation. Under strict liability, producers still would bear some risk because of incomplete liability insurance coverage, but under negligence, neither producers nor consumers now would bear any risk.

Consumers Can Take Care

An important simplifying assumption in the discussion thus far has been that the consumer cannot affect her expected accident loss by taking care. This assumption obviously is not realistic in some product liability situations. For example, the probability that a soda bottle will cause harm certainly depends on how it is handled by the purchaser. If the consumer can affect the expected loss by taking care, then the efficient solution to the accident problem also will involve her taking some appropriate level of care. Although the analysis of this issue is similar to the analysis of the pedestrian's care decision

75. The discussion in this paragraph presumes that the incompleteness of coverage under liability insurance is comparable to that under first-party accident insurance. If this is not the case, then the different degrees of coverage also would have to be taken into account.

in the automobile accident example in Chapter 6,[76] there are some important differences because of the possibility considered here that the victim misperceives the expected accident loss.

Under strict liability, a defense of contributory negligence is required to get the consumer to take appropriate precautions. Assuming the consumer meets the standard of care, the producer will be liable for the consumer's losses and the earlier discussion of strict liability in this chapter will be applicable. However, if the consumer underestimates the probability or magnitude of the harm, she will underestimate the value of meeting the standard of care applicable to her. If, as a result, she does not meet the standard, she would bear her own losses. Consequently, the producer would not have an incentive to take care. Moreover, because the consumer underestimates her expected loss, she might not be willing to buy first-party accident insurance even if the premium equals her expected loss.

Under a negligence rule, the producer will take appropriate care in order to avoid liability, so the consumer will bear the loss. If the consumer underestimates the expected loss, she generally will not take the desired level of precautions and may not purchase first-party accident insurance. Thus, when consumers can affect expected accident losses by taking care, but underestimate these losses, neither strict liability with a defense of contributory negligence nor negligence may be ideal with respect to the care exercised by the parties or with respect to the allocation of risk.

The discussion in this chapter has been premised on the assumption that the victim of the product accident is the purchaser of the product. In some product accident situations, however, the victim may be a *third party*. For example, a defective lawnmower may throw a rock that hits a bystander rather than the lawnmower owner. When the victim is a third party, the argument for using the rule of strict liability is

76. See pp. 47-50 above.

strengthened relative to the argument for using the rule of negligence. The reason is straightforward. Under strict liability, the price of the product will equal its full cost, including the expected accident losses *to third parties*. Consumers therefore will purchase the correct amount. Under negligence, the price will not reflect the expected accident losses to third parties because producers will choose not to be negligent. And because consumers do not suffer the harm, they will ignore these losses when deciding how much of the good to purchase. Consequently, they will buy too much. This problem is not different in kind from the one that occurred when the victim was a consumer. But then, at least to the extent that the consumer perceived the magnitude of the expected loss, she would in effect add that amount to the price of the good. Thus, the problem with the negligence rule — that it encourages too much output — generally is worse when the victim is a third party.

It should be clear by now that the preferred liability rule for dealing with product accidents depends on several, possibly conflicting, considerations. If the victims are consumers of the product and if they have perfect information about the product risks, then the rule of strict liability with a defense of contributory negligence and the rule of negligence can induce both producers and consumers to take appropriate care and can induce consumers to purchase the correct amount of the product. If consumers underestimate expected accident losses, however, then only strict liability with a defense of contributory negligence will achieve these results, *provided* that consumers meet the standard of care applicable to them. But because of their imperfect information, they might not perceive the value of meeting this standard. If they do not meet it, then even strict liability with a defense of contributory negligence will be inefficient.

Once considerations of risk allocation are added to the above discussion, matters become even more complicated (unless ideal insurance is available). If insurance is not available or if it is imperfect because of the problem of moral hazard, then, generally speaking, strict liability becomes more desirable relative to negligence to the extent that the victims are more risk averse than the producers, and vice versa. When all of the effects of product liability rules are taken into account — on the producers' care, on the victims' care, on industry output, and on risk allocation — it is clear that, in general, no one rule will be best in every respect. What rule should be used depends on the relative importance of these competing considerations in each type of products liability situation.

CHAPTER 15

TENTH APPLICATION — PRINCIPAL-AGENT LIABILITY

In all of the preceding applications it has been assumed, implicitly, that the injurer is a single actor.[77] In many instances, however, a harm is caused by an individual who is under the control of someone else. A driver of a truck making deliveries for a pizza company might hit a pedestrian, or a worker employed by a factory might fail to build an item that the factory was contractually obligated to supply. These examples illustrate a situation in which an "agent" — the driver or the worker — causes harm while under the supervision of a "principal" — the pizza company or the factory.

In this chapter we will reexamine some of the principles of liability from earlier chapters when the harm is caused by the agent of a principal. The primary questions to be addressed are: Is the optimal level of liability different when harm is caused by an agent of a principal rather than by a single actor? Should liability be imposed on the principal, the agent, or both? If on both, what is the optimal mix of liability between the principal and the agent?

Basic Analysis

To answer these questions we will reconsider the pollution control example from Chapter 13, treating the firm as the

---

77. This was true even when we discussed firms, which were treated as if they were single actors.

principal and the firm's employees as agents. For simplicity, assume that the only cost of production is the cost of labor. Each employee produces one unit of output per day and either does or does not filter the waste byproduct. Pollution damage is $40 if the waste is not filtered and $10 if it is. If employees are not liable for pollution damage, they would have to be paid, given their alternative employment opportunities, $100 a day if they don't filter the waste and $115 if they do — the extra $15 compensates them for the disutility of dealing with the waste (assume it has an awful smell).[78] Thus, if employees are not liable for pollution damage, the firm's production cost per unit of output would be $100 if employees don't filter the waste and $115 if they do. The full cost of the product — the firm's production cost plus the victims' pollution damage — therefore is $140 if the waste is not filtered ($100 of labor cost plus $40 of damage), and $125 if it is filtered ($115 of labor cost plus $10 of damage). These numbers are the same ones used in Chapter 13. As there, the efficient solution involves filtering the pollution before discharging it (filtering reduces damages by $30 at a cost of only $15), and consumption of the good only by individuals who value it at $125 or more per unit (its full cost given that filtering is undertaken).

It is assumed that the governing legal rule is strict liability. First consider imposing liability for pollution damage on the firm. The data for this case are described in Table 15. If the firm does not require its employees to filter the waste, the firm will have to pay them $100 a day, and it will bear $40 in liability costs for each unit produced. Therefore, its total cost per unit would be $140. If the firm does require filtering, it will have to pay its employees $115 a day and it will bear $10 in liability costs, for a total cost per unit of $125. Clearly, if the firm is liable for pollution damage, it will require its employees to filter, since its total costs will be lower as a result. In a competitive market, moreover, the firm will sell its output for $125 a unit because that price corresponds to

---

78. In other words, the assumption is that the employees could find other jobs for which they would be paid $100 a day and neither have to deal with pollution nor bear any risk of liability.

TABLE 15

Principal-Agent Example — Firm is Strictly Liable

Behavior of Employee	Firm's Production (Labor) Cost Per Unit	Firm's Liability Cost Per Unit	Firm's Total Cost Per Unit
	(1)	(2)	(3)
Don't filter	$100	$40	$140
Filter	$115	$10	$125

its unit costs. Hence, strict liability on the firm will lead to the efficient outcome.

Now suppose, instead, that employees are strictly liable for the pollution damage. The data for this case are described in Table 16. If an employee does not filter the waste, he will bear $40 in liability costs. To induce him to work for the firm, then, the firm would have to pay him $140 a day — $100 for his time and effort, plus $40 to compensate him for bearing the cost of liability. If the firm paid him less than this, he would choose alternative employment.[79] If the employee does filter the waste, he will bear $10 in liability costs. The firm then would have to pay him $125 a day — $115 for his time and effort and the unpleasantness of dealing with the waste, plus $10 to compensate him for bearing the cost of the liability. Note that, if employees are liable for the pollution damage, they would be indifferent between (a) receiving compensation of $140 a day and not filtering the waste, and (b) receiving compensation of $125 a day and filtering the waste. In both cases they obtain $100 a day for their time and effort, plus compensation for bearing any other disutility (dealing with the wast, if they filter) or cost (their liability cost).

The firm, however, would prefer that employees filter the waste, since the firm's production cost — which is its only cost in the present case because it is not liable — is lower. Since the employees are indifferent between filtering and not

79. See the preceding footnote.

TABLE 16

Principal-Agent Example — Employee is Strictly Liable

Behavior of Employee	Firm's Production (Labor) Cost Per Unit (1)	Firm's Liability Cost Per Unit (2)	Firm's Total Cost Per Unit (3)
Don't filter	$40	$140	$140
Filter	$10	$125	$125

filtering, provided they are compensated appropriately, they will be willing to do what the firm desires. Thus, if employees are strictly liable for damages, they will filter the waste and receive $125 a day from the firm. The firm will sell its output for $125 a unit because that corresponds to its unit costs (in this case, solely labor costs). Hence, making the employees strictly liable also will lead to the efficient outcome.

This example illustrates two general points. First, aside from some qualifications discussed below, it does not matter whether liability is imposed on the agent or on the principal.[80] The reason in essence is that any liability imposed on the agent will lead the agent to demand higher wages (in order to be willing to bear this liability), which means that the principal will bear the liability indirectly through this wage adjustment. As we observed in the example above, the principal's incentives to control the agent's behavior are the same whether the principal bears liability directly, or indirectly by having to pay higher wages.

The irrelevance of the assignment of liability also holds if liability is split between the principal and the agent, provided that the total level of liability is unchanged. Suppose, for example, that the principal is liable for half of the harm and the agent is liable for the other half. The principal would indirectly

---

80. This result can be viewed as another application of the simple (zero transaction cost) version of the Coase Theorem, in which the efficient outcome will occur regardless of the choice of legal rule.

bear the liability imposed on the agent by having to increase the agent's compensation (though by less than if the agent were fully liable for the harm). Because the principal will incur this cost, together with the principal's direct liability for half of the harm, the principal will bear the full cost of the harm — just as if the principal were fully liable for the harm or the agent were fully liable for the harm (and demanded correspondingly higher wages).

The second general point illustrated by the example is that the optimal level of liability, however allocated between the principal and the agent, is the level of harm. We observed in earlier chapters that when the injurer is a single actor, the optimal level of liability equals the harm because, if the injurer is forced to internalize the harm, he will have the appropriate incentive to take precautions. The same is true in a principal-agent setting, essentially for the same reason. If the principal internalizes the harm — whether directly by bearing liability or indirectly by having to pay higher wages to the agent for bearing liability — the principal will have an incentive to direct the agent to take efficient precautions (filtering the waste, in our example). But if the level of liability differs from the harm, the principal generally would direct the agent to take precautions that are inefficient — excessive precautions if liability is too high, and inadequate precautions if liability is too low.[81] Notably, imposing liability on both the principal and the agent for the harm — so that total liability equals twice the harm — would lead to excessive precautions being taken.

Agent Risk Aversion

Three refinements of the preceding analysis are worth mentioning. The first concerns the possibility that the agent

---

81. Consider, for example, what would happen if the agent were made liable for pollution damage but the level of liability equals one-quarter of the harm. Then the agent would bear liability of $10 if he does not filter (1/4 × $40) and $2.50 if he does (1/4 × $10). The principal therefore would have to pay the agent $110 a day if the agent does not filter ($100 + $10) or $117.50 a day if he does filter ($115 + $2.50). Thus, the principal would instruct the agent not to filter.

is risk averse. (The principal could be risk averse, too, but this case is less interesting, so for simplicity we will assume that the principal is risk neutral.) In the pollution control example above, there was no risk because harm was certain to occur. But agent risk aversion would be relevant if the harm is accidental in character, such as in the products liability application. Agent risk aversion also would be relevant if the agent's malfeasance can be detected only with some probability, for then the sanctioning of the agent is uncertain.

For reasons analogous to those discussed in several of the prior applications, including breach of contract remedies and automobile accidents, the risk aversion of a party generally lowers the optimal level of liability that it should bear. The same conclusion applies here. If risk-averse agents are made liable whenever an uncertain harm occurs, the amount they should pay is less than the harm, due to the fact that the agents' bearing of risk is a cost that can be reduced by lowering the level of their payment.

Paradoxically, the preceding statement does not affect the main conclusions about principal-agent liability that we reached in the basic analysis above. There we concluded that the optimal level of liability is equal to the harm and that it does not matter whether this level of liability is imposed on the principal, the agent, or a combination of the two. This conclusion still holds even if the agent is risk averse, for the following reason.

If liability for an uncertain harm is imposed on the agent, the principal will have an incentive to indemnify the agent to reduce the agent's bearing of risk. Otherwise, the agent would demand higher compensation, not only for the expected liability cost, but also for the bearing of risk per se. Conversely, if liability for harm is imposed on the principal alone, the principal will be reluctant to impose an internal sanction on the agent because such a sanction would result in the agent's demanding higher compensation. In other words, whether liability is imposed on the agent or on the principal, the principal will want to insulate the agent from risk in order to lower the principal's wage cost. Moreover, if the level of liability equals the harm caused, the principal will continue to be properly motivated to induce the agent to take cost-effective precautions, for the reasons discussed in the basic analysis.[82]

Monitoring of Agents

The second refinement of the basic analysis concerns the possibility that, in many principal-agent contexts, it may be difficult to determine whether an agent engaged in conduct that caused harm. For example, if pollution is emitted from a firm, it might not be obvious who in the firm was responsible for this occurring. If a factory breaches its contract to supply a good in a timely manner, it may be hard to figure out which employee caused the delay. Clearly, in these kinds of situations, imposing liability directly on the agent is problematic, if not impossible. Similarly, it may be difficult for the principal to levy internal sanctions on the agent for conduct that resulted in harm.

But liability still can be imposed on the principal. If the principal is made strictly liable for the harm, she will have the appropriate incentive to monitor and control her agents, for example, by requiring them to keep detailed records of their activities or by hiring other individuals to observe the agents' performance. Additionally, even if the direct observation of agents' conduct is not feasible or economical, making the principal strictly liable for harm will motivate her to impose internal sanctions that are not explicitly tied to agent conduct, such as reducing agents' compensation whenever harm occurs (regardless of its cause), to encourage agents to act appropriately.

In sum, if it is not feasible to make agents directly liable for harm because their harm-creating conduct is difficult to observe, it still is desirable to make the principal liable for harm, to give the principal proper incentives to control her

---

82. If the principal can costlessly observe the agent's behavior, as was assumed implicitly in the basic analysis, the principal would contract with the agent to eliminate the agent's bearing of risk, while still directing the agent to take cost-effective precautions.

agents in any way she can. Moreover, even if the principal couldn't influence the behavior of her agents, imposing liability on the principal is beneficial because this will cause the principal to reduce her participation in harm-creating activities. For example, if the principal is a firm that is polluting, making the firm liable for harm will cause the price of the firm's product to rise to reflect its full cost, which will cause less of the product to be purchased and less pollution to occur.

The Judgment-Proof Problem

The third refinement of the basic analysis concerns the possibility that the agent is judgment proof — that is, does not have assets sufficient to pay for the harm that his actions might cause. A judgment-proof agent will tend to take inadequate precautions to prevent harm. Instead of comparing his cost of preventing harm to the benefit of preventing harm, he will compare his cost to some lesser amount — the amount for which he can be made liable. Consequently, a precaution that is desirable — whose cost of prevention is less than the harm — might not be viewed by the agent as worth taking. This conclusion is consistent with our observation in earlier chapters that actors who cause harm generally should have to pay for the harm, to properly motivate them to reduce harm.[83]

In many circumstances, even though an agent may be judgment proof, the principal will be capable of paying for the harm caused. This often would be true, for example, when the agent is an employee and the principal is a firm. In this situation, agent liability and principal liability are no longer equivalent. If liability is imposed solely on the agent, the agent will take insufficient precautions to prevent harm because the agent will bear only a fraction of the harm. It would be preferable to impose liability on the principal. While the principal

---

83. In theory, the judgment-proof problem could be solved by making the agent's compensation conditional on his taking proper care, but this would require that the principal be able to easily observe and direct the agent's conduct, which often will not be feasible in practice.

also will find it difficult to properly motivate a judgment-proof agent, there are two advantages to making the principal liable rather than the agent, analogous to those discussed at the end of the preceding section. First, having to pay for the full harm will give the principal an appropriate incentive to find ways to better control the agent. Second, even if the principal can't prevent the agent from taking insufficient care, having to pay for the full harm will cause the principal to appropriately reduce her participation in harm-creating activities.

Whenever harm is caused by an agent of a principal —such as by an employee of a firm — the question naturally arises whether liability should be imposed on the principal or on the agent. Under the assumptions made in the basic analysis in this chapter, principal liability and agent liability are equivalent. Moreover, the optimal level of liability equals the harm regardless of which form of liability is used. We also observed that these results hold whether the agent is risk neutral or risk averse. If agent liability is problematic because courts cannot easily determine whether an agent was responsible for causing harm, imposing liability on the principal will give the principal the correct incentive to monitor, and possibly sanction, her agents, as well as to reduce her participation in harm-creating activities. Similarly, if the agent is judgment proof, liability should be imposed on the principal. For these reasons, principal liability often will be superior to agent liability in practice.

CHAPTER 16

ELEVENTH APPLICATION — SUIT, SETTLEMENT, AND TRIAL

In most of the preceding applications, the focus of the discussion has been on the choice of a substantive legal rule, such as whether an injurer should be made strictly liable or liable only if negligent. The process used to enforce these rules — that is, the litigation process — was ignored. It was assumed implicitly that the victim of the harm could cost-lessly sue the injurer and that the victim would prevail at trial with certainty. We will now examine the victim's decision to bring a suit — and the parties' incentives to settle the case out of court — when litigation is costly and the trial outcome is uncertain. We also will consider how the litigation process affects the analysis of substantive legal rules.

The Litigation Process

The litigation process will be analyzed through an example involving a dispute between a *plaintiff* (the victim) and a *defendant* (the injurer) over the loss of $10,000. The numerical values used in the example — the rest of which will be discussed below — are summarized in Table 17. It is assumed initially that both parties are risk neutral.

The plaintiff will have some belief about the probability of her prevailing if she sues the defendant and the case goes to trial. Suppose for concreteness that she thinks that she has an 80 percent chance of winning at trial. Then the plaintiff's *expected* winnings at trial are $8,000 (an 80 percent chance

TABLE 17

Litigation Process Example

Amount in dispute:

$10,000

Plaintiff's belief about the probability that she will prevail at trial:

80%

Plaintiff's litigation costs:

$3,000

Plaintiff's expected net winnings at trial:

$5,000 = (80% × $10,000) − $3,000

Defendant's belief about the probability that the plaintiff will prevail at trial:

80% (when plaintiff and defendant agree)[a]

Defendant's litigation costs:

$3,000

Defendant's expected total payment at trial:

$11,000 = (80% × $10,000) + $3,000

Size of settlement range:

$6,000 = $11,000 − $5,000

a. This probability is assumed to be 90 percent when the plaintiff is pessimistic relative to the defendant, and 10 percent when the plaintiff is optimistic relative to the defendant.

of winning $10,000). Assuming that she has to pay for her own litigation costs, the plaintiff will bring a suit against the defendant only if her litigation costs are less than $8,000. For example, if the plaintiff's litigation costs are $3,000, she will sue — and her net benefit from the suit will be $5,000 (the expected winnings of $8,000 less the litigation costs of $3,000). In general, therefore, a risk-neutral plaintiff will bring a suit if her expected winnings at trial exceed her litigation costs.

Most suits that are brought are settled out of court for an obvious reason — settlements save the cost of litigation.[84] To illustrate this motivation for a settlement, suppose in the example that the defendant agrees with the plaintiff's assessment of the plaintiff's probability of prevailing at trial. In other words, suppose the defendant also believes that the plaintiff has an 80 percent chance of winning. Then the defendant's expected liability to the plaintiff is $8,000 (an 80 percent chance of having to pay $10,000). Assuming that the defendant also bears $3,000 in litigation costs, his expected total payment is $11,000 ($8,000 + $3,000).

It is now easy to see why the parties have a strong motivation to settle the case out of court. If a trial occurs, the plaintiff's expected net gain is $5,000 and the defendant's expected total payment is $11,000. Any out-of-court settlement in which the defendant pays the plaintiff at least $5,000 but less than $11,000 makes both parties better off than going to trial. Note that the size of the settlement range is $6,000 (the difference between $5,000 and $11,000), which corresponds to the *sum* of the parties' litigation costs ($3,000 each). This example illustrates the following general conclusion from the economic analysis of litigation: If the parties agree about the plaintiff's probability of prevailing at trial, there always exists a range of out-of-court settlements that can make both of them better off; the size of this range is determined by the sum of their litigation costs.

In practice, the parties are unlikely to have the same beliefs about the probability that the plaintiff will prevail at trial. Their disagreements often are attributable to the different sources of information that they rely on. For example, the defendant's superior knowledge about his own conduct would lead him to assess the chance of his being found negligent differently from the plaintiff. (Similarly, the plaintiff may have a different estimate than the defendant of the probability that she will be found contributorily negligent.) Given a disagree-

---

84. Although some costs also are incurred in the process of settling a case, these costs generally are substantially less than the costs of going to trial. For simplicity, settlement costs will be ignored.

ment, there are two cases to consider, depending on whether the plaintiff is *optimistic* or *pessimistic* about her chance of prevailing at trial relative to the defendant's beliefs about the plaintiff's chance.

Suppose first that the plaintiff is pessimistic relative to the defendant. For example, suppose the plaintiff thinks, as before, that she has an 80 percent chance of winning, but that the defendant thinks the plaintiff has a 90 percent chance of prevailing.[85] It is easy to see that plaintiff pessimism increases the likelihood of a settlement. The plaintiff's expected net gain from trial remains at $5,000, but the defendant's expected total payment increases to $12,000 (a 90 percent chance of paying $10,000, plus $3,000 in litigation costs). Thus, while the plaintiff still will demand at least $5,000 to settle the case, the defendant now can pay up to $12,000 (instead of $11,000) and be better off than going to trial. Note that the size of the settlement range, which is $7,000 (the difference between $5,000 and $12,000), now exceeds the sum of the parties' litigation costs. Everything else equal, plaintiff pessimism increases the settlement range.

Suppose, alternatively, that the plaintiff is optimistic relative to the defendant. For example, let the plaintiff continue to believe that her chance of winning is 80 percent, but let the defendant think that the plaintiff's chance of prevailing is only 10 percent. This degree of plaintiff optimism makes a settlement impossible. As before, the plaintiff will demand at least $5,000 to settle the case. But the defendant's expected payment at trial falls to $4,000 (a 10 percent chance of paying $10,000, plus $3,000 in litigation costs). Because the defendant will not be willing to pay more than $4,000 to settle the case, and the plaintiff will not accept less than $5,000, there is no

---

85. In constructing this example, it is immaterial that the plaintiff's beliefs remain constant and the defendant's beliefs change. What matters is that the plaintiff thinks she has a worse chance of winning than the defendant thinks she has. Also, because the term "pessimism" is used in this relative sense, it is possible, as in the example, for the plaintiff to be "pessimistic" even when she believes that she is likely to win. (Observations analogous to those in this note apply to the case of plaintiff optimism discussed below.)

way that a settlement can be reached. The settlement range has disappeared. In general, plaintiff optimism reduces the settlement range and even can eliminate it, as happened in the example here.

This analysis of the settlement process can be summarized in the following way. If the parties agree about the plaintiff's probability of prevailing at trial, or if the plaintiff is pessimistic relative to the defendant, a settlement range always exists. This range is at least as large as the sum of the parties' litigation costs and increases with the degree of the plaintiff's pessimism. However, if the plaintiff is relatively optimistic about winning, a settlement range may not exist. The greater the plaintiff's optimism, the more likely is this outcome to occur.

Thus far it has been assumed that the plaintiff and the defendant are risk neutral. That assumption may be reasonable in some cases, especially when the amount at stake is small relative to each party's net worth. In many disputes, however, the parties will be risk averse. Taking risk aversion into account will affect the analysis of the litigation process in two ways.

The first effect is to reduce the plaintiff's incentive to sue. This is because a risk-averse plaintiff, by definition, will value a suit at less than her expected winnings at trial. In effect, she will subtract a "risk premium" from the expected winnings to account for her dislike of the uncertainty of the trial outcome.[86] Thus, a suit that would have been brought by a risk-neutral plaintiff might not be brought by a risk-averse one.

The second effect of risk aversion is to increase the parties' incentives to settle cases out of court. Because a settlement eliminates the risk that would be borne by both parties if they were to go to trial, the more risk averse they are, the stronger will be their preference for settling a case. Thus, because of risk aversion, a case that otherwise would have gone to trial might now be resolved by a settlement.

---

86. Recall from Chapter 10 that the term "risk premium" refers to a risk-averse individual's dislike of risk per se. See p. 83 above. There, in the context of law enforcement, a risk premium was added to the expected fine. Here, a risk premium is subtracted from the expected winnings. In both cases, the risk premium makes a risk-averse individual worse off.

To illustrate this possibility, consider the earlier example in which the plaintiff's optimism about winning at trial eliminated the settlement range. The risk-neutral plaintiff had an expected net gain from trial of $5,000 and would not settle for less, while the risk-neutral defendant faced an expected total payment of $4,000 and would not offer more. Suppose now, however, that the plaintiff is risk averse and would be willing to accept $3,500 with certainty rather than bear the uncertainty associated with going to trial. Similarly, suppose that the defendant is risk averse and would be willing to offer $5,500 with certainty to avoid the unknown trial outcome. (In other words, the plaintiff subtracts a risk premium of $1,500 from her expected net gain and the defendant adds a risk premium of $1,500 to his expected total payment.) Risk aversion has changed the situation from one in which a settlement is impossible to one in which any settlement between $3,500 and $5,500 is preferred to trial by both parties. In general, risk aversion increases the settlement range and can even create one, as happened in the example here.

One final consideration relevant to the settlement process should be noted — strategic behavior. As was seen in the context of nuisance law in Chapter 4, if the parties to a dispute behave strategically, they might not be able to reach an agreement that would make them better off.[87] Similarly, one should not assume here that a settlement necessarily will occur whenever a settlement range exists. During the settlement negotiations, each party has an incentive to act strategically so as to obtain a settlement within the settlement range that is more favorable to himself. If a bargaining failure occurs — say because of bluffing — the parties may end up going to trial. Thus, while a settlement range is necessary before a settlement can be reached, it does not guarantee a settlement.

The discussion of the litigation process in this section has shown that there are two benefits from settling cases out of court — avoiding the cost of litigation and removing the uncertainty of the trial outcome. The discussion also has shown that there are two reasons why cases might not be settled

87. See pp. 20-21 above.

despite these benefits. If the plaintiff is optimistic relative to the defendant, a settlement range may not exist. And even if a settlement range exists, strategic behavior may prevent the parties from reaching a settlement.

The Analysis of Substantive Legal Rules

As previously noted, the analysis of substantive legal rules in this book implicitly assumed that whenever someone suffered harm she could costlessly sue the injurer and she would prevail at trial with certainty. To see how a costly and uncertain litigation process affects the analysis of a substantive legal rule, we will reconsider the rule of strict liability in the context of driver-pedestrian accidents.

In the simplest version of the automobile accident example, the parties were risk neutral and only the driver's care — represented by the driver's speed — affected the pedestrian's expected accident cost. Whenever an accident occurred, the loss was $10,000; higher speed resulted in a greater likelihood of an accident. We saw that the rule of strict liability, with liability equal to the victim's loss, led the driver to drive at the socially desired speed.[88]

Now suppose that the same numerical values used in Table 17 apply to the automobile accident example — specifically, that the driver and pedestrian agree that the pedestrian's chance of prevailing at trial is 80 percent, and that each side will incur $3,000 in litigation costs. If the driver's liability is set equal to the pedestrian's loss of $10,000, the pedestrian will bring a suit because her expected winnings at trial ($8,000) exceed her litigation costs ($3,000). It is assumed for simplicity that the pedestrian's suit results in a trial. (The possibility of a settlement will be considered briefly later.)

First note that taking the litigation process into account may alter the socially desired speed of the driver. As in the earlier discussions of the automobile accident example, the

---

88. The statements in this paragraph are based on the discussions at pp. 43-46 and 71-72 above.

TABLE 18

Automobile Accident Example — Driver's Care Affects Expected Accident Cost and Litigation Costs Are Included

Behavior of Driver	Benefit to Driver	Expected Accident Cost to Pedestrian	Expected Litigation Cost	Benefit Minus Cost
Drive rapidly	$120	$100	$60	−$40
		(= 1/100 × $10,000)	(= 1/100 × $6,000)	
Drive moderately	$80	$40	$24	$16
		(= 1/250 × $10,000)	(= 1/250 × $6,000)	
Drive slowly	$50	$20	$12	$18
		(= 1/500 × $10,000)	(= 1/500 × $6,000)	

efficient outcome requires that the driver act so as to maximize total benefit less total cost. But now total cost includes both the expected accident cost to the pedestrian *and* the expected litigation cost of both parties.

The parties' expected litigation costs can be easily calculated. Whenever an accident occurs, a suit will result and $6,000 will be spent by the parties on litigation. As in Chapter 9, suppose the probability of an accident is 1/100 if the driver drives rapidly, 1/250 if he drives moderately, and 1/500 if he drives slowly.[89] Then total expected litigation cost is $60 if the driver drives rapidly (1/100 × $6,000), $24 if he drives moderately (1/250 × $6,000), and $12 if he drives slowly (1/500 × $6,000).

The data for the simple version of the automobile accident example were contained in Table 3, which is reproduced here as Table 18 with the addition of the total expected litigation costs. The last column now represents the benefit to the driver less the expected accident cost to the pedestrian and less the parties' expected litigation cost. Given the data in Table 18,

89. See p. 72 above.

the efficient outcome is for the driver to drive slowly. Recall that in Table 3, when litigation costs were assumed implicitly to be zero, it was efficient for the driver to drive at moderate speed.[90] Thus, the presence of litigation costs causes the efficient speed of the driver to fall. This should not be surprising because, in effect, the cost of an accident has risen by the cost of litigation; it therefore is desirable for the driver to take more care.[91]

Now consider how fast the driver will choose to drive, given his belief that the pedestrian has an 80 percent chance of prevailing at trial and that the trial will cost the driver $3,000 in litigation costs. The driver will choose the speed that maximizes his benefit net of his expected liability payment and net of his expected litigation cost. If he drives rapidly, his benefit is $120 (see Table 18), his expected liability payment is $80 ($1/100 \times 80\% \times \$10,000$), and his expected litigation cost is $30 ($1/100 \times \$3,000$). Thus, his net benefit is $10 ($120 − $80 − $30). It is straightforward to compute that his net benefit is $36 if he drives moderately ($80 − $32 − $12) and $28 if he drives slowly ($50 − $16 − $6). Consequently, the driver will choose to drive at moderate speed — too fast relative to the speed that is desired when litigation costs are taken into account.

The driver drives faster than is socially desirable in this example for two related reasons. First, because the pedestrian's chance of prevailing at trial is less than 100 percent, the driver is led to ignore some of the expected harm that he imposes on the pedestrian. Second, because the driver only has to pay for his own litigation cost, he also is led to ignore the litigation cost borne by the pedestrian. In essence, the rule of strict liability fails in this example to induce efficient behavior because it does not force the driver to consider all of the adverse effects his behavior has on the pedestrian.

Thus far, it has been taken for granted that the driver's

90. See pp. 43-44 above.
91. This explanation is correct provided that there is a suit whenever there is an accident. However, for reasons discussed at pp. 144-145 below, it may be advantageous to set the level of liability low enough to discourage suits.

liability at trial equals the pedestrian's loss of $10,000. In the analysis of strict liability in Chapter 6, where the litigation process was implicitly assumed to work without cost and without error, it was seen that setting liability equal to the victim's loss *was required* in order to get the injurer to behave properly.[92] However, if victims are not assured of prevailing at trial, or if litigation costs are present, it may be desirable for the level of liability to be greater than or less than the victim's loss.

It is easy to see in the present example that raising the level of liability above the pedestrian's $10,000 loss can improve matters. Because the driver has an 80 percent chance of losing at trial, if the driver's liability is set at $10,000, his expected liability will be $8,000 — less than the pedestrian's loss. But if the driver's liability at trial is increased to $12,500, his expected liability will be $10,000 (80% × $12,500); the driver then will take all of the pedestrian's harm into account. In a similar way, the level of liability at trial can be raised in order to make the driver also take the pedestrian's litigation costs into account. With these upward adjustments of the level of liability, the driver can be induced to drive slowly, a socially preferred outcome (see the last column of Table 18).

There also is a potential rationale for lowering the level of liability when litigation is costly — to discourage suits and thereby reduce litigation costs. To see this point in the automobile accident example above, consider how different levels of liability will affect the pedestrian's incentive to sue. Given an 80 percent chance of prevailing at trial and $3,000 in litigation costs, the pedestrian will bring a suit as long as the judgment at trial exceeds $3,750 (because 80 percent of any amount higher than $3,750 exceeds $3,000).

Suppose the judgment is set below this level in order to discourage suits. If the driver knows that he will not be sued, he will drive rapidly because his benefit is greatest when he drives rapidly. Given the data in Table 18, his benefit then is $120 and the pedestrian's expected accident cost is $100. Because there are no litigation costs (there are no suits), the

92. See p. 45 above.

social net benefit is $20 ($120 − $100). Note that this outcome is superior to the driver being sued and driving slowly, for then the social net benefit is $18 (see Table 18). Although discouraging suits causes the driver to take less care, the resulting savings in litigation costs more than make up for the driver's less desirable behavior.

This discussion shows that determining the optimal level of liability is more complicated when one takes the litigation process into account. In some situations, it will be preferable to raise the level of liability above the victim's loss so that the injurer will respond to all of the costs that he imposes on the victim. But in other situations, it may be better to lower the level of liability in order to discourage suits and reduce litigation costs, even though this will result in the injurer taking less care.

There are additional aspects of the litigation process that make the analysis of substantive legal rules more complex. Consider, for example, the possibility that cases will settle out of court. Obviously, to the extent that cases settle, the parties' expected litigation costs will be lower. But if a settlement is acceptable to the injurer, it must be because it is preferred to the expected trial outcome; thus, settlements will reduce the cost to the injurer of engaging in harm-creating behavior and generally will cause the injurer to take less care.

Although a complete analysis of a substantive legal rule would have to incorporate these and other complications, the methodology would be the same as that used in this section: In determining what the efficient outcome is, it is necessary to include not only the direct benefits and costs of the parties (such as the driver's benefit from driving and the pedestrian's expected accident cost), but also their litigation costs. And in evaluating how well a substantive legal rule achieves efficiency, it is necessary to take into account the plaintiff's incentive to sue and the defendant's response to being sued.

This chapter has provided an overview of the economic analysis of litigation. Although the first section focused on an abstract dispute between a plaintiff and a defendant, and the second section reconsidered the driver-pedestrian example, the observations developed here apply to any substantive legal rule enforced by the victim of the harm — including all of the rules previously discussed in the context of the nuisance law, breach of contract, automobile accident, pollution control, and products liability applications.

In passing, it is worth noting one similarity and one difference between the private litigation process discussed in this chapter and the public law enforcement problem analyzed in Chapter 10. The principal rationale there for using fines that exceed the harm caused was that the injurer could escape detection with some probability; a similar rationale applies here when the plaintiff's chance of prevailing at trial is less than 100 percent. With public law enforcement, the level of the fine and the amount spent on enforcement can be set independently; however, in the private litigation process, the level of the defendant's liability determines the extent of enforcement (whether a suit will be brought and how much will be spent by the parties on litigation).

CHAPTER 17

EFFICIENCY AND EQUITY RECONSIDERED

The discussion of efficiency and equity in Chapter 2 showed that there is no conflict between these goals if income can be redistributed costlessly. In essence, this is because any inequity in the distribution of income caused by the pursuit of efficiency could be corrected at no cost. The assumption that redistribution is costless was made at the end of that chapter. We will now reconsider this assumption, first with respect to the redistribution of income by means of the government's tax and transfer system and then with respect to redistribution by the choice of legal rules.

Redistribution by Taxes and Transfers

In general, the redistribution of income by taxes or transfers is costly in the following sense. Recall from the discussion in Chapter 12 that if the price of a good equals its cost of production, only those individuals who value the good more than its cost will purchase it. This was seen to be efficient. The good used to illustrate this point in Chapter 12 was a lawnmower that cost $100 to produce. Suppose that rich people are more likely to purchase lawnmowers than poor people because they are more likely to live in houses than in apartment buildings. Then, by imposing an excise tax on purchasers of lawnmowers, the government would raise more tax revenue from the rich than from the poor. Assuming that the revenue is spent in a way that does not disproportionately favor the rich — say it benefits everyone equally — then the net effect of the tax would be to redistribute income from the rich to the poor. However, an inevitable byproduct of this redistribution is that the price of lawnmowers will be "distorted" — that is, the effective price of lawnmowers, including the tax, will exceed their cost of production. As a consequence, too few lawnmowers will be bought. For example, if the excise tax is $10 per lawnmower, then everyone who values a lawnmower more than the production cost of $100 but less than $110 will not purchase one, an inefficient outcome given that they value the good more than its cost of production. In general, to redistribute income by an excise tax it is necessary to sacrifice some efficiency with respect to consumption decisions. This loss of efficiency is a cost of redistributing income.[93]

The same kind of problem applies to income taxes, although not in as obvious a way. To see the distortion from income taxes, first note that leisure is a commodity desired by consumers just like any other commodity. The "price" of an hour of leisure is the income forgone by not working that hour. For example, suppose that the wage rate in the widget industry is $25 per hour and that widget workers have some flexibility with regard to the number of hours they work. If widget workers did not have to pay income taxes, then they would give up $25 to consume an hour of leisure. Thus, those individuals who valued another hour of leisure more than $25 would "buy" more leisure by working an hour less. But suppose widget workers faced a 20 percent income tax. Then for every hour worked, they would pay $5 to the government and retain $20. The "price" of leisure therefore would fall to $20 per hour. Now individuals who value leisure more than $20 per hour will work less.[94] Assuming that the $25 per hour wage

93. There are also, of course, administrative costs incurred in implementing any tax (or transfer) system.

94. Actually, this statement might not be correct. To see why, suppose an individual's preferences are such that he wants to consume a particular bundle of goods and services before consuming any leisure. Then the imposition of an income tax will *increase* the number of hours he has to work to be able to purchase these goods and services. Whether individuals increase or decrease the number of hours they work does not affect the general point that this example will be used to illustrate.

reflects a worker's contribution to the value of the widgets produced, the income tax will cause an inefficient consumption decision regarding leisure. For example, a worker who values leisure at $21 per hour will work less even though the value of the worker's time in terms of widget production is $25 per hour. As in the case of the excise tax, the income tax distorts the price of some commodity — in this case leisure — and causes inefficient consumption decisions. Thus, it too imposes a cost in order to redistribute income.

Redistributing income by transfers rather than by taxes does not avoid the problem of distorting consumption decisions. For instance, suppose the government subsidizes the price of electricity for low-income individuals. Then the individuals who receive the subsidy will face an effective price of electricity that is below the cost of producing electricity and therefore will buy too much of it relative to what is efficient.[95] In general, any kind of tax or transfer used to redistribute income will distort the price of some commodity and will have this kind of efficiency cost.

Can Legal Rules Redistribute Income?

Given the cost of redistributing income by taxes and transfers, the question naturally arises whether the legal system should be used to redistribute income. That legal rules *can* be used to redistribute income was suggested by the discussion in Chapter 3 of the distributional aspects of the Coase Theorem.[96] In the example in that chapter — of the factory polluting the residents — recall, for example, that when there were no transaction costs, the choice between the right to pollute and the right to clean air redistributed income by the $150 cost of the smokescreen (the least-cost solution to the conflict). It does not follow from that discussion, however, that legal rules

---

95. This statement obviously presumes that electricity would otherwise be priced according to its cost. In practice, however, electricity might not be priced this way because of government regulation.

96. See pp. 14 and 15 above.

always affect the distribution of income. To understand why, it will be useful to distinguish between legal disputes in which the parties are in some kind of contractual relationship, including a market relationship, and disputes in which the parties are, in effect, "strangers" prior to the dispute. The breach of contract and products liability examples would be characterized as *contractual disputes*, while the nuisance law, automobile accident, and pollution control examples would be described as *disputes between strangers*. (The products liability example is of the first type because the victim is a consumer; it would be of the second type if the victim were a third party.) It will be shown below that legal rules often cannot redistribute income in contractual disputes, whereas legal rules always can redistribute income in disputes between strangers.

To see why it is frequently difficult, if not impossible, to use legal rules to redistribute income in contractual disputes, reconsider the discussion in Chapter 5 of breach of contract. In the example used there, the seller of widgets might want to breach the contract with the initial buyer if an offer from a third party materialized. Suppose it is desirable for equity reasons to redistribute income from the seller to the buyer. Giving the buyer the remedy of expectation damages makes the buyer as well off if the contract is breached as he would have been had it been performed. Giving the buyer the remedy of reliance damages or restitution damages makes the buyer worse off if the contract is breached. However, because the contract price the buyer and seller negotiate depends on what the remedy is, it does not follow that the buyer is better off with the expectation remedy. Clearly, the seller will demand a higher price and the buyer will be willing to pay more if the buyer receives a larger payment in the event of a breach. Thus, considering both the higher initial contract price and the higher compensation in the event of a breach, the buyer may not be any better off with the expectation remedy. In general, the parties will take any distributional effects of breach of contract remedies into account when they negotiate the contract price; thus, how the joint benefits of entering into the contract are shared between the parties depends primarily, if not exclusively, on their relative bargaining strengths, not on the remedies available to them.

An analogous observation can be made about the products liability application when the victim of the product accident is a consumer of the good. Suppose, for example, that it is desirable for equity reasons to redistribute income from producers to consumers. It was seen in Chapter 14 that under the rule of negligence, producers will meet the standard of care and, therefore, consumers will bear their own losses. But under the rule of strict liability, consumers will be fully compensated for their losses (assuming, if there is a defense of contributory negligence, they meet the standard of care applicable to them). Consumers will not, however, be better off as a class under strict liability because, in a competitive long-run equilibrium, the price of the good will rise by an amount equal to the producers' expected liability.[97] In general, then, whenever the parties to a dispute are in some kind of contractual or market relationship, it may be difficult, if not impossible, to use the legal system to redistribute income.

To see why legal rules can be used to redistribute income in disputes between strangers, reconsider the discussion of automobile accidents in Chapter 6. In the simplest version of the example employed there, the pedestrian's expected accident losses depended solely on whether the driver chose to drive slowly, moderately, or rapidly. Under a negligence rule, the pedestrian will bear her own losses because the driver will choose to meet the standard of care — to drive moderately — whereas under a strict liability rule the driver will have to compensate the pedestrian for her losses. Because there is no contractual or market relationship between the parties, there is no contract price or market price that can be adjusted when legal rules change. Thus, shifting from one liability rule to the

97. However, if the market for the product is not competitive, then consumers *may* be better off as a class under strict liability. Because it is beyond the scope of this book to consider markets that are not competitive (see note 63 above), this point will not be considered further.

other will redistribute income by the amount of the expected losses.[98]

Analogous observations can be made with respect to the nuisance law and pollution control applications. In the nuisance example discussed in Chapter 4 — of a polluting factory next to a single resident — the choices of the entitlement and the remedy for protecting the entitlement have distributional consequences. Given the entitlement, a party generally is better off if it is protected by an injunctive remedy rather than by a damage remedy (with liability equal to actual damages); although the damage remedy guarantees that the protected party will be fully compensated for damages, the injunctive remedy gives that party the right to hold out for more. And under either remedy, a party obviously is better off if the entitlement is more favorable to that party.

In the pollution control example in Chapter 13, in which the pollution victims are third parties, the distributional effects of choosing between strict liability and negligence to control the polluting industry are similar to those discussed in the automobile accident context. Under negligence, the victims bear their own losses, whereas under strict liability the producers — and ultimately consumers of the product — bear these losses. In general then, whenever the parties to a dispute are "strangers" — that is, not in a contractual or market relationship — the choice of legal rules will have distributional consequences.

Should Legal Rules Be Used to Redistribute Income?

Having now identified the types of situations in which the legal system is most likely to have distributional effects, we can return to the question of whether legal rules *should* be used in these situations to promote distributional equity.

98. If, as discussed in Chapter 9, the parties are risk averse and the driver can buy liability insurance or the pedestrian can buy first-party accident insurance, the redistribution will take the form of allocating the insurance premium to one party or the other rather than the risk of bearing the pedestrian's losses.

The answer to this question depends in part on the "cost" of using legal rules to redistribute income relative to the cost of using taxes or transfers.

There are two senses in which redistribution through the legal system may be costly. The first relates to the administrative costs of using the legal system. Suppose, for example, that the consumers of the goods produced by some polluting industry are high-income individuals, while the victims living near the polluting factories are low-income individuals. By making the firms strictly liable for the pollution damage, income will be transferred from rich people to poor people. A similar transfer could be accomplished by taxing high-income individuals and transferring the proceeds to low-income persons. The tax and transfer system is a *much* less expensive way to redistribute income than is the legal system. Roughly speaking, to transfer a dollar through a private lawsuit from a defendant to a plaintiff costs on average about a dollar in administrative costs, including the litigation costs of both parties and the costs of the court system. To transfer a dollar through the tax and transfer system costs only a fraction of this amount.

Legal redistribution also may be costly in a second sense: Inefficient rules may have to be chosen in order to achieve the desired result. For example, recall the discussion in Chapter 9 of driver-pedestrian accidents in which both parties are risk averse and the pedestrian cannot affect expected losses. It was seen that negligence is efficient because the driver will meet the standard of care and the pedestrian will be able to buy a first-party accident insurance policy with full coverage; strict liability may not be efficient because of the moral hazard problem (which could result in the driver not being able to buy a liability insurance policy with full coverage and/or in the driver not taking appropriate care). But if drivers are wealthier than pedestrians, strict liability may be preferable to negligence on equity grounds. The loss of efficiency from using strict liability rather than negligence is a "cost" of redistributing income from drivers as a class to pedestrians as a class.

There may be instances in which redistribution through

the legal system is not costly in this sense. For example, suppose that in some types of nuisance disputes the parties can be expected to bargain in a cooperative way. Then, for the reasons discussed in Chapter 4, any entitlement will lead to the efficient outcome, whether protected by an injunctive remedy or a damage remedy. Thus, the choices of the entitlement and the remedy can be used to redistribute income without causing an inefficient resolution of the nuisance dispute. In general, however, not all legal rules will be efficient, so it often may be necessary to choose an inefficient legal rule in order to promote equity.

An additional consideration in deciding whether to use the legal system to promote distributional equity is the "precision" of legal redistribution. Legal rules will not be able to redistribute income systematically unless the status of the parties in a certain type of dispute corresponds closely to the groups between which redistribution is desired. For example, in automobile accidents involving drivers and pedestrians, there probably is not a close correspondence between the income of a party and whether that party is a driver or a pedestrian. It may be that higher income persons are more likely to be drivers than pedestrians, but certainly there are many low-income drivers and high-income pedestrians. Thus, liability rules regarding driver-pedestrian accidents are not very precise instruments for accomplishing income redistribution. In nuisance and pollution control disputes, there may be a closer correspondence between the income of a party and whether that party is a victim or an injurer. The purchasers of the goods produced by some polluting industry may be mainly higher-income people, while the victims of the pollution may be primarily lower-income persons. Thus, in some kinds of disputes, the choice of a legal rule might contribute toward the implementation of distributional goals.

Even when there is a close correspondence between the status of the parties in a certain kind of dispute and the groups between which redistribution is desired, legal rules still might not be able to achieve redistribution as systematically as an income tax system. This is because redistribution through the legal system only may occur when a dispute arises, and not all members of a given income class will be involved in a dispute. For instance, even if the goods produced by a polluting industry were consumed exclusively by rich persons and the pollution victims were all poor people, not every rich person necessarily purchases this commodity and not every poor person lives near a factory in this industry. Thus, the legal rule used to control the pollution dispute will, at best, redistribute income from a subset of one income class to a subset of another.[99] In sum, the legal system is not nearly as precise as the tax system in redistributing income among income classes.

The initial discussion of efficiency and equity in Chapter 2 showed that, if it is costly to redistribute income, there may be a tradeoff between efficiency and equity. In other words, it may be desirable to choose an inefficient policy in order to promote the desired distribution of income. The present chapter has shown that income redistribution generally *is* costly, whether it is accomplished by the tax and transfer system or by the legal system. Nonetheless, several reasons have been suggested in this chapter why the choice of legal rules should be based primarily on efficiency considerations. In some circumstances — contractual disputes — legal rules often will have little or no effect on the distribution of income. In situations in which the legal system does have distributional consequences — disputes between strangers — legal rules still should be based primarily on efficiency considerations because legal rules generally are more costly than taxes and transfers as a means of redistributing income and less precise. Thus, the justification for the assumption made at the end of

99. The point of this example may not be fully applicable in some legal contexts. For example, consider driver-pedestrian accidents and suppose that drivers would purchase liability insurance if strict liability is chosen and pedestrians would purchase first-party accident insurance if negligence is chosen. Then, even though only a fraction of all drivers and only a fraction of all pedestrians may be involved in an accident, the choice between strict liability and negligence will affect everyone because of insurance. The point of the pollution example in the text then would apply only to the extent that the insurance coverage is incomplete.

Chapter 2 — that income could be redistributed without cost — is not only that this simplified the subsequent exposition by allowing us to focus on the efficiency analysis of legal rules. As this chapter has shown, the justification also is that, even when the cost of redistributing income is taken into account, there are reasons why the efficiency analysis should be of principal importance.

CHAPTER 18

A SUMMING UP

Now that we have completed the discussion of the relationship between efficiency and equity and have examined several applications of the efficiency criterion to legal rules, the major themes of the book can be summarized. These themes will be presented in the form of three questions that generally should be considered in an economic analysis of a legal rule. The first question is concerned with choosing the criterion for evaluating legal rules. The second and third questions are concerned with determining the effectiveness of legal rules in satisfying the criterion. As these questions are discussed below, the reader should refer to Figure 1, which shows the relationships among them.

The Efficiency-Equity Question

Should efficiency be the sole criterion used to evaluate legal rules, or should equity be taken into account as well? Because this question has just been answered at length in the previous chapter, not much needs to be said here. In disputes in which the parties are in a contractual or market relationship — as in the breach of contract and products liability examples — efficiency usually should be the only criterion; this is because it is very difficult, if not impossible, to redistribute income through the choice of legal rules applicable to these kinds of disputes. In disputes in which the parties are, in actuality or in effect, strangers — as in the nuisance law, automobile accident, and pollution control examples — it is possible to promote the equitable distribution of income through

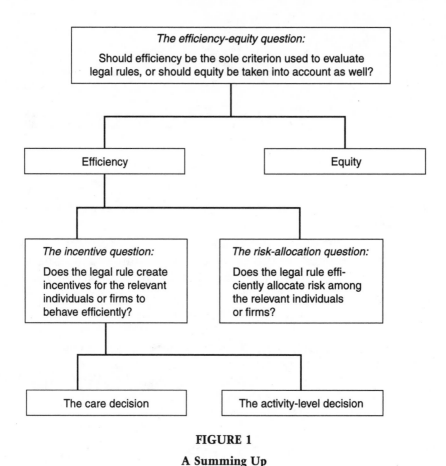

FIGURE 1

A Summing Up

the legal system, but this usually can be done better through the government's tax and transfer system. Thus, efficiency generally should be the primary criterion for evaluating legal rules. Given this criterion, there are two key aspects of efficiency that determine the extent to which legal rules satisfy the criterion: incentives and risk allocation.

The Incentive Question

Does the legal rule create incentives for the relevant individuals or firms to behave efficiently? "Efficient behavior" here means behavior that maximizes aggregate benefits less aggregate costs. Because individuals and firms naturally consider the effects of their behavior on their own benefits and costs, the incentive problem for legal rules is how to induce individuals and firms to take into account the effects of their behavior on the benefits and costs of others. There are two aspects of behavior that are encompassed within the incentive question: the *care decision* and the *activity-level decision*.

The *care decision* generally refers to the behavior of an individual or a firm that affects costs and benefits, *aside from* the individual's or the firm's level of participation in the activity that is the source of the dispute. (What is meant by "level of participation in the activity" will become clear below.) The term *care* applies most naturally to the automobile accident and products liability examples, in which care corresponds, for example, to how fast the driver drives, to whether the pedestrian walks or runs, and to whether the soda manufacturer uses bottles or cans. It also readily applies to the pollution control example, in which care corresponds to whether the polluter filters or not.

The term *care* is meant, however, to apply more generally. In the nuisance law example, because the output of the factory is assumed to determine the amount of pollution, care can refer either to the factory's output or to the amount of pollution. In the breach of contract example, care corresponds both to the seller's decision whether to breach when a third-party offer is made and to the buyer's investment in reliance. And in the first law enforcement example, care corresponds to the residents' decisions whether to double park. In these examples, the legal system was evaluated in terms of whether it created incentives for individuals or firms to take the appropriate amount of care.

The *activity-level decision* generally refers either to the number of individuals or firms that choose to participate in the activity that is the source of the dispute, or to the extent of each individual's or firm's participation in such an activity. Among the applications we have discussed, this decision arose explicitly only in the automobile accident, pollution control, and products liability examples. In the automobile accident example, the driver's activity level corresponded to how much he drove, which affected his own benefits and the expected accident costs. In the pollution control and products liability examples, the activity level corresponded to the output of the industry. This was determined by consumers' decisions about how much of the good to purchase, which affected their own benefits and, respectively, pollution damages or expected accident costs. Thus, in these examples, legal rules were evaluated both in terms of whether they created incentives for the parties to take the appropriate amount of care and in terms of whether they created incentives for the parties to engage in the harm-creating activity at an appropriate level.[100]

In general, therefore, the incentive aspect of efficiency will encompass both a care decision and an activity-level decision, and legal rules should be evaluated with respect to their effects on both decisions. We now can turn to the second key aspect of efficiency.

The Risk-Allocation Question

Does the legal rule efficiently allocate risk among the relevant individuals or firms? We saw in the discussion of risk bearing and insurance in Chapter 7 that it is desirable to reduce the risk borne by a risk-averse party. This is true whether the risk is a beneficial one (when the uncertainty is about how much one will gain) or a detrimental one (when the uncertainty is about how much one will lose). If the risk cannot be (or is not) eliminated, then it should be allocated among the relevant individuals or firms according to their relative aversion to risk. This may mean that the risk should be shared among the

---

100. The activity-level issue also could have been discussed in the nuisance law application, which was based on an example of a polluting factory next to a single resident. As noted in the previous paragraph, because the factory's output was assumed to determine the amount of pollution, output or pollution can be treated interchangeably as representing the factory's care. If we had considered the effects of nuisance remedies on the *number* of factories locating near the pollution victim, there also would have been an activity-level issue.

parties, or shifted entirely to one of them, or, if relevant, shifted to an insurance company.

The risk-allocation issue was discussed in the context of the breach of contract, automobile accident, products liability, and law enforcement examples. In the first example, we saw how the remedies for breach of contract allocate the beneficial risk of a higher third-party offer between the seller and the buyer. In the automobile accident and products liability examples, we saw how liability rules allocate the detrimental risk of an accident between the injurer (a driver or a manufacturer, depending on the example) and the victim (a pedestrian or a consumer). And in the law enforcement example concerning fines, we saw how the risk-bearing costs of an enforcement system are determined by the choice of how much to invest in detecting violators and how much to fine them. In each example, the legal system was evaluated in terms of how well it promoted the optimal allocation of risk.

The goal of reducing risk-bearing costs by compensating victims of accidents sometimes is confused with the goal of promoting distributional equity. The source of this confusion is easiest to see in the context of the automobile accident example. Suppose that the driver is risk neutral, and that the pedestrian is risk averse but cannot obtain first-party accident insurance. There is then an efficiency argument for using the rule of strict liability to compensate the pedestrian for her losses. This argument is based on risk-allocation considerations, not equity considerations. However, using the rule of strict liability rather than the rule of negligence also has distributional consequences. In effect, it redistributes the expected accident losses from the class of pedestrians to the class of drivers. Whether this is desirable in terms of equity is a separate matter. In general, there is an efficiency basis for using the legal system to reduce the bearing of risk. The resulting distributional effects should be evaluated separately.

In thinking about both the risk-allocation question and the incentive question, it also is important to consider the relationship between private insurance and legal rules. As seen in the context of the automobile accident and products liability examples, if an ideal insurance policy is available — that is, a policy with full coverage and a premium that reflects the insured party's expected losses — then the legal system does not need to take risk-allocation concerns into account. However, if the policy does not provide complete coverage, then it may be desirable to base legal rules in part on risk-allocation considerations. Also, if the premium does not reflect expected losses, the policy might adversely affect the incentives of the insured party. This is the moral hazard problem, first discussed in Chapter 7. In general, therefore, the optimal choice of legal rules to deal with incentive and risk-allocation issues may depend on the availability and nature of private insurance.

This summary of the themes of the book highlights a point that already has been seen in some of the specific applications: The legal system generally cannot accomplish all of the objectives we have considered. Tradeoffs may have to be made between promoting efficiency and promoting equity. Even if efficiency is the only goal, there may be a conflict between incentive issues and risk-allocation issues. And even if only incentive considerations are relevant, a legal rule may not be able to simultaneously induce efficient care decisions and efficient activity-level decisions. However, as we have seen in specific applications, the inability of the legal system to achieve every objective does not mean that the economic approach to law is necessarily indeterminate and unhelpful. To the contrary, the fact that there are many goals that the legal system might be viewed as trying to accomplish makes economic analysis all the more helpful in determining what the tradeoffs are among the goals and how to strike an appropriate balance.

CHAPTER 19

CONCLUSION

As noted in the introduction, the goal of this book has been to convey a sense of how to "think like an economist" about legal rules and policies. To accomplish this, many simplifying assumptions have been made, and the legal system intentionally has been described in a somewhat abstract way. In this concluding chapter, some of the practical difficulties in employing economic analysis to study law will be discussed.

The Problem of Valuation

Probably the most difficult problem in undertaking an economic analysis of a legal rule is putting dollar values on the relevant costs and benefits. These dollar values should be determined by the affected individuals (provided one accepts the principle of consumer sovereignty discussed briefly at the end of Chapter 2). It is easy to infer the value an individual would place on a cost or benefit if the loss or gain involves a standardized good that is sold in a market. The value is simply the price of the good. For example, suppose that in a breach of contract dispute a buyer's loss consists solely of having to repurchase in the marketplace a good that was supposed to have been delivered by some particular seller. This loss is easily valued by the price of the good at the time of breach (plus any incidental costs associated with the transaction). However, the valuation process is much more difficult if the loss or gain involves a nonstandardized or unique good. For instance, suppose that as a result of pollution someone is forced to move from his home. Although the market price of the home could be determined from the sales prices of similar homes, this price will not reflect the special attachment the person who lived there may have had for that location and house.

In situations in which the losses or gains involve nonmarketed or nonstandardized items, one could in principle ask the affected individual how much he values the loss or gain. However, this approach is hindered by the obvious problem that losers often would have an incentive to overstate their losses — for example, if their compensation is based on their stated losses. Similarly, gainers may have an incentive to understate their gains.

Moreover, even if it were possible to overcome these problems, there would be the following ambiguity. With respect to a loss, should the loser be asked "How much would you be willing to pay to avoid the loss?" or "How much would you have to be paid to allow the loss to be imposed on you?" The answers to these questions generally are not the same. For example, suppose that you are a very noise-sensitive person involved in a dispute with your neighbor over the loudness of her stereo and that you have little wealth — say $5,000. You might be willing to pay a large fraction of your wealth — say $3,000 — for quiet, but you might not accept less than $10,000 to allow her noise to be imposed on you. In deciding whether to assign an entitlement to noise or quiet (or some intermediate entitlement), should a court treat the value of quiet as $3,000 or $10,000? The same kind of ambiguity would arise in valuing gains.

These ambiguities are due to what economists call *wealth effects*. Wealth effects occur in situations in which a person places a high value, relative to his wealth, on the loss or gain in question. To see what is meant by a wealth effect, note that the question "How much would you be willing to pay to avoid the loss?" implicitly assumes that you will suffer the loss unless you pay to avoid it, whereas the question "How much would you have to be paid to allow the loss to be imposed on you?" implicitly assumes that you will not suffer the loss. If you value the loss highly, then you are, in effect, much poorer when you are asked the first question than when you are asked the second. It is not surprising, then, that the answer to the first question is less than the answer to the second. This is why the ambiguity is said to be due to a wealth effect. If the loss in question is not an "important" one in this sense, then the answers to the two questions will be very close to each other and the ambiguity will, for all practical purposes, disappear. In general, however, these two questions will produce different answers.

Because of the above difficulties, the practical implementation of economic analysis usually will require a somewhat arbitrary method to determine the value of losses and gains involving nonmarketed or nonstandardized items. There are many procedures that have been developed by economists to estimate these values. For instance, it may be possible to infer the value placed on quiet by examining how much more homes in quiet neighborhoods sell for, everything else equal (everything else can be held equal by statistical methods). The values derived from this procedure obviously reflect a representative or average person's values. Thus, the value of quiet for an especially noise-sensitive person will be understated, and vice versa. In practice, any procedure used to estimate dollar values for costs or benefits will make some mistakes of this kind.

The problem of assigning dollar values to costs and benefits is particularly difficult when bodily harm is involved. An individual presumably would give up all of his wealth to avoid the certainty of being killed and would not accept any amount of money to volunteer to be killed. The same may be true with respect to the loss of limbs. Thus, it might seem that economic analysis cannot deal with situations in which life or limb is involved. If this were true, it would especially constrain the economic analysis of law because many legal disputes involve bodily harm.

However, the fact that individuals would not voluntarily sacrifice life or limb for any amount of money is not directly relevant to situations in which life or limb is at risk. The relevant question then is "How much would you be willing to pay to reduce the *probability* of bodily harm?" or "How much would you have to be paid to accept an increase in the probability of bodily harm?" These are questions that individuals implicitly answer every day. They frequently are willing to pay more to fly rather than to drive, not only because it is faster, but also because it is safer. Similarly, many laborers are willing to work in riskier industries in part because of the higher wages they can obtain. Although any procedure used to infer the value of life or limb from data of this sort will be somewhat arbitrary because of the problems discussed above, there is no fundamental reason why economic analysis cannot be employed to evaluate legal rules that affect the risk of bodily harm.

Despite what has been said, there undoubtedly will be instances in which it will be very difficult or impossible to arrive at reasonable values for certain costs or benefits. While this problem arises with the use of economic analysis generally, it may be especially relevant to the economic analysis of law because legal disputes often involve losses or gains that are difficult to value. Some critics of economic analysis have suggested that the problem of valuation may lead to a bias in the economic approach, in that the categories of costs or benefits that are hard to quantify will tend to be ignored. Other critics have suggested that because of the difficulty of quantifying certain costs or benefits, the economic analyst will tend to substitute his own subjective values for these items, and therefore the analysis may simply "confirm" his prior beliefs. Both of these arguments may have merit in some instances. But they should be seen as potential criticisms of economic *analysts* rather than of economic *analysis.* The analyst should be careful to consider all relevant costs and benefits, including those hard to value. He also should be careful to state his assumptions and methods explicitly so that others can decide whether prior beliefs or careful analysis have determined the conclusion. Despite these potential problems, economic analysis has been found to be very helpful in the design of public policy in many areas. There is no fundamental reason why it should not be just as useful in the examination of the legal system.

BIBLIOGRAPHICAL APPENDIX

As in the earlier editions, the primary purpose of the appendix is to provide a guide to the law and economics literature on which this book is based, and a secondary purpose is to identify some articles that develop ideas closely related to those contained in the book. Accordingly, the main change to the bibliographical appendix in the present edition is the addition of references relevant to the new chapters on imprisonment and principal-agent liability. I have not changed the citations applicable to the chapters that appeared in the first and second editions except to update them — to newer editions of books and to published versions of articles that previously were available only in unpublished form.

As noted in the Preface, I also have simplified the bibliographical appendix by omitting from the guide to additional law and economics reading many of the early books and journal symposia listed in the first and second editions. In lieu of this material, the present edition contains an updated overview of this literature, mainly referring to the leading textbooks and treatises in the field of law and economics, as well as to several comprehensive bibliographical guides to the literature that have been published since the second edition.

The points made in the chapter on the Coase Theorem derive from Ronald H. Coase's classic article, The Problem of Social Cost, 3 J.L. & Econ. 1 (1960). Since this article was published, dozens of articles have been written about it. The ones that are most relevant to this book are concerned with the effects of strategic behavior on the bargaining process. See, for example, Donald H. Regan, The Problem of Social Cost Revisited, 15 J.L. & Econ. 427, 427-432 (1972), and Robert Cooter, The Cost of Coase, 11 J. Legal Stud. 1, 14-29 (1982).

The chapter on nuisance law draws heavily on A. Mitchell Polinsky, Resolving Nuisance Disputes: The Simple Economics of Injunctive and Damage Remedies, 32 Stan. L. Rev. 1075 (1980).[101] That paper builds on the foundation laid by Guido Calabresi and A. Douglas Melamed in their path-breaking article, Property Rules, Liability Rules and Inalienability: One View of the Cathedral, 85 Harv. L. Rev. 1089 (1972). For other closely related discussions of these issues, see, for example, Frank I. Michelman, Pollution as a Tort: A Non-Accidental Perspective on Calabresi's *Costs*, 80 Yale L.J. 647, 669-673 (1971), Robert C. Ellickson, Alternatives to Zoning: Covenants, Nuisance Rules, and Fines as Land Use Controls, 40 U. Chi. L. Rev. 681, 738-748 (1973), and Richard A. Posner, Economic Analysis of Law 60-63, 67-71 (6th ed. 2003).

The results described in the first chapter on breach of contract remedies — in which the parties are assumed to be risk neutral — are developed formally in an important article by Steven Shavell, Damage Measures for Breach of Contract, 11 Bell J. Econ. 466 (1980). For extensions of this analysis, see William P. Rogerson, Efficient Reliance and Damage Measures for Breach of Contract, 15 Rand J. Econ. 39 (1984), and Steven Shavell, The Design of Contracts and Remedies for Breach, 98 Q.J. Econ. 121 (1984). The second chapter on breach of contract remedies — which focuses on risk-allocation issues — follows closely the discussion in A. Mitchell Polinsky, Risk Sharing Through Breach of Contract Remedies, 12 J. Legal Stud. 427 (1983).[102] For some related analyses, see Lewis A. Kornhauser, Reliance, Reputation, and Breach of Contract, 26 J.L. & Econ. 691, 701-702 (1983), and Steven Shavell, The Design of Contracts and Remedies for Breach, 98 Q.J. Econ. 121, 127-128,

130, 146-147 (1984). Other relevant discussions of breach of contract include those by John H. Barton, The Economic Basis of Damages for Breach of Contract, 1 J. Legal Stud. 277 (1972), Charles J. Goetz & Robert E. Scott, Liquidated Damages, Penalties and the Just Compensation Principle: Some Notes on an Enforcement Model and a Theory of Efficient Breach, 77 Colum. L. Rev. 554 (1977), and Richard A. Posner, Economic Analysis of Law 93-143 (6th ed. 2003).

The first chapter on automobile accidents was concerned both with the care exercised by the parties and with the extent of their participation in the relevant activity. The discussion of the care issue derives generally from the pioneering article by John Prather Brown, Toward an Economic Theory of Liability, 2 J. Legal Stud. 323 (1973), while the discussion of the activity-level issue is based on Steven Shavell, Strict Liability Versus Negligence, 9 J. Legal Stud. 1 (1980). See also Peter A. Diamond, Single Activity Accidents, 3 J. Legal Stud. 104 (1974). The second chapter on automobile accidents — which focuses on risk-allocation and insurance issues — derives generally from Steven Shavell, On Liability and Insurance, 13 Bell J. Econ. 120 (1982). For some other discussions of accident law of related interest, see, for example, Guido Calabresi, The Costs of Accidents: A Legal and Economic Analysis (1970), Guido Calabresi, Optimal Deterrence and Accidents, 84 Yale L.J. 656 (1975), and Richard A. Posner, Economic Analysis of Law 167-213 (6th ed. 2003).

The first part of the chapter on law enforcement using fines — in which the individuals whose behavior is being controlled are assumed to be risk neutral — develops ideas first formalized in a classic paper by Gary S. Becker, Crime and Punishment: An Economic Approach, 76 J. Pol. Econ. 169 (1968). Some closely related discussions include those by George J. Stigler, The Optimum Enforcement of Laws, 78 J. Pol. Econ. 526 (1970), Richard A. Posner, Economic Analysis of Law 215-247 (6th ed. 2003), and A. Mitchell Polinsky & Steven Shavell, The Optimal Use of Fines and Imprisonment, 24 J. Pub. Econ. 89 (1984). The second part of the chapter — in which the individuals are assumed to be risk averse — is based generally on A. Mitchell Polinsky & Steven Shavell, The Optimal Tradeoff Between the Probability and Magnitude of Fines, 69 Am. Econ. Rev. 880 (1979). For an application of some of the ideas in this chapter to antitrust enforcement, see Kenneth G. Elzinga & William Breit, The Antitrust Penalties: A Study in Law and Economics 112-138 (1976), and Michael K. Block & Joseph Gregory Sidak, The Cost of Antitrust Deterrence: Why Not Hang a Price Fixer Now and Then?, 68 Geo. L.J. 1131 (1980).

The chapter on law enforcement using imprisonment is based primarily on A. Mitchell Polinsky & Steven Shavell, On the Disutility and Discounting of Imprisonment and the Theory of Deterrence, 38 J. Legal Stud. 1 (1999). The economic analysis of imprisonment as a sanction is much less well developed than that of fines. For an early contribution see Michael K. Block & Robert C. Lind, An Economic Analysis of Crimes Punishable by Imprisonment, 4 J. Legal Stud. 479 (1975). More recent analyses of imprisonment as a sanction include A. Mitchell Polinsky & Steven Shavell, The Optimal Use of Fines and Imprisonment, 24 J. Pub. Econ. 89 (1984), Louis Kaplow, A Note on the Optimal Use of Nonmonetary Sanctions, 42 J. Pub. Econ. 245 (1990), Richard A. Posner, An Economic Theory of the Criminal Law, 85 Colum. L. Rev. 1193 (1985), and Steven Shavell, Criminal Law and the Optimal Use of Nonmonetary Sanctions as a Deterrent, 85 Colum. L. Rev. 1232 (1985). The point that fines should be used to the fullest extent possible before resorting to imprisonment was made by Gary S. Becker, Crime and Punishment: An Economic Approach, 76 J. Pol. Econ. 169, 193-198 (1968).

The basic idea developed in the chapter on pollution control is implicit in an article by Guido Calabresi, Some Thoughts on Risk Distribution and the Law of Torts, 70 Yale L.J. 499, 500-507 (1961), and is stated more explicitly by Richard B. Stewart & James E. Krier, Environmental Law and Policy: Readings, Materials and Notes 227 (2d ed. 1978). It is formalized in A. Mitchell Polinsky, Strict Liability vs. Negligence in a Market Setting, 70 Am. Econ. Rev.: Papers & Proc. 363 (1980). An essentially identical discussion is contained in an article by Steven Shavell, Strict Liability Versus Negligence, 9 J. Legal Stud. 1, 3, 14 (1980).

The analysis of strict liability in the chapter on products liability derives generally from an important article by A. Michael Spence, Consumer Misperceptions, Product Failure and Producer Liability, 44 Rev. Econ. Stud. 561 (1977). Spence's analysis was expanded to include negligence in a paper by Steven Shavell, Strict Liability Versus Negligence, 9 J. Legal Stud. 1, 3-5, 14-16 (1980). Other closely related discussions include those by Dennis Epple & Artur Raviv, Product Safety: Liability Rules, Market Structure, and Imperfect Information, 68 Am. Econ. Rev. 80 (1978), and A. Mitchell Polinsky & William P. Rogerson, Products Liability, Consumer Misperceptions, and Market Power, 14 Bell J. Econ. 581 (1983).

The chapter on principal-agent liability is not based on any particular article, but derives generally from literature on the economics of principal-agent relationships that is well known. Although most of this literature is not concerned with the imposition of liability and sanctions in a principal-agent setting, there are several articles that do address this topic. Some early contributions include Lewis A. Kornhauser, An Economic Analysis of the Choice Between Enterprise and Personal Liability for Accidents, 70 Calif. L. Rev. 1345 (1982), Note, An Efficiency Analysis of Vicarious Liability Under the Law of Agency, 91 Yale L.J. 168 (1981), and Alan O. Sykes, The Economics of Vicarious Liability, 93 Yale L.J. 1231 (1984). For a more recent article on this topic, see Harry A. Newman & David W. Wright, Strict Liability in a Principal-Agent Model, 10 Intl. Rev. L. & Econ. 219 (1990).

The first half of the chapter on suit, settlement, and trial — discussing the litigation process — is based on ideas associated with William M. Landes, An Economic Analysis of the Courts, 14 J.L. & Econ. 61, 62-69, 101-102 (1971), John P. Gould, The Economics of Legal Conflicts, 2 J. Legal Stud. 279, 284-293 (1973), and Richard A. Posner, An Economic Approach to Legal Procedure and Judicial Administration, 2 J. Legal Stud. 399, 417-420 (1973). This early work was ably synthesized and extended by Steven Shavell in Suit, Settlement, and Trial: A Theoretical Analysis Under Alternative Methods for the Allocation of Legal Costs, 11 J. Legal Stud. 55 (1982). See also Richard A. Posner, Economic Analysis of Law 567-571, 581-

593 (6th ed. 2003). Much of this literature was subsequently reexamined using the economic theory of games with asymmetric information. For two early examples of this approach, see I. P. L. P'ng, Strategic Behavior in Suit, Settlement, and Trial, 14 Bell J. Econ. 539 (1983), and Lucian Arye Bebchuk, Litigation and Settlement under Imperfect Information, 15 Rand J. Econ. 404 (1984). See also Robert Cooter & Thomas Ulen, Law and Economics 373-426 (3d ed. 2000).

The second half of the chapter on suit, settlement, and trial — discussing how the litigation process affects the analysis of substantive legal rules — derives generally from A. Mitchell Polinsky & Daniel L. Rubinfeld, The Welfare Implications of Costly Litigation for the Level of Liability, 17 J. Legal Stud. 151 (1988). A companion piece focusing on settlements is A. Mitchell Polinsky & Daniel L. Rubinfeld, The Deterrent Effects of Settlements and Trials, 8 Intl. Rev. L. & Econ. 109 (1988). Other articles that formally consider how the litigation process affects the theory of liability include Janusz A. Ordover, Costly Litigation in the Model of Single Activity Accidents, 7 J. Legal Stud. 243 (1978), Steven Shavell, The Social versus the Private Incentive to Bring Suit in a Costly Legal System, 11 J. Legal Stud. 333 (1982), and I. P. L. Png, Litigation, Liability, and Incentives for Care, 34 J. Pub. Econ. 61 (1987). For two broad surveys of the literature on the economics of litigation, see Steven C. Salop & Lawrence J. White, Economic Analysis of Private Antitrust Litigation, 74 Geo. L.J. 1001, 1016-1039, 1053-1064 (1986), and Robert Cooter & Daniel L. Rubinfeld, Economic Analysis of Legal Disputes and Their Resolution, 27 J. Econ. Lit. 1067 (1989).

Because the purely economic topics dealt with in the book — efficiency and equity, risk bearing and insurance, and competitive markets — are all standard fare for students of economics, the discussions of these topics are not based on particular articles.

The more specific issue of whether legal rules can and should be used to redistribute income has been discussed by several authors. For example, the general point that legal rules can redistribute income more easily in noncontractual situations than in contractual ones is made by Harold Demsetz,

Wealth Distribution and the Ownership of Rights, 1 J. Legal Stud. 223 (1972). A similar point is made with respect to product liability rules by Koichi Hamada, Liability Rules and Income Distribution in Product Liability, 66 Am. Econ. Rev. 228 (1976). Whether legal rules should be used to redistribute income has been discussed in general terms by, among others, Steven Shavell, A Note on Efficiency vs. Distributional Equity in Legal Rulemaking: Should Distributional Equity Matter Given Optimal Income Taxation?, 71 Am. Econ. Rev.: Papers & Proc. 414 (1981), and A. Mitchell Polinsky, Economic Analysis as a Potentially Defective Product: A Buyer's Guide to Posner's *Economic Analysis of Law*, 87 Harv. L. Rev. 1655 (1974).[103] The redistributive function of legal rules also has been discussed in specific legal contexts by, for example, Bruce A. Ackerman, Regulating Slum Housing Markets On Behalf of the Poor: Of Housing Codes, Housing Subsidies and Income Redistribution Policy, 80 Yale L.J. 1093 (1971), Anthony T. Kronman, Contract Law and Distributive Justice, 89 Yale L.J. 472 (1980), Guido Calabresi & A. Douglas Melamed, Property Rules, Liability Rules and Inalienability: One View of the Cathedral, 85 Harv. L. Rev. 1089 (1972), and A. Mitchell Polinsky, Resolving Nuisance Disputes: The Simple Economics of Injunctive and Damage Remedies, 32 Stan. L. Rev. 1075 (1980). See also Richard A. Epstein, The Social Consequences of Common Law Rules, 95 Harv. L. Rev. 1717 (1982).

One of the issues discussed in the concluding chapter of the book was the difficulty of valuing gains and losses when there are wealth effects. This issue was first highlighted in a legal context by Ezra J. Mishan, Pareto Optimality and the Law, 19 Oxford Econ. Papers 255 (1967). It continues to receive attention. See, for example, Duncan Kennedy, Cost-Benefit Analysis of Entitlement Problems, 33 Stan. L. Rev. 387 (1981). Another issue discussed in the concluding chapter was the difficulty of valuing life and limb. Many approaches to this

---

103. My current views about the appropriateness of using the legal system to redistribute income — which are explained in Chapters 2 and 17 of this book — differ somewhat from the views reflected in this and other earlier articles. In brief, I now see a more limited role for distributional considerations in the choice of legal rules and policies.

problem have been developed by economists. For a survey of some of them, see, for example, Michael W. Jones-Lee, The Value of Life: An Economic Analysis (1976). The concluding chapter also referred to critics of economic analysis who argue either that categories of costs or benefits that are difficult to quantify will tend to be ignored, or that the economic analyst will tend to substitute his own subjective values for these costs or benefits. For some discussions of this sort, see, for example, Laurence H. Tribe, Policy Science: Analysis or Ideology?, 2 Phil. & Pub. Aff. 66 (1972), Frank I. Michelman, Norms and Normativity in the Economic Theory of Law, 62 Minn. L. Rev. 1015 (1978), and Mario J. Rizzo, The Mirage of Efficiency, 8 Hofstra L. Rev. 641 (1980).

Addendum to the Third Edition: The literature in law and economics has grown tremendously since the second edition. Rather than trying to provide a comprehensive "reader's guide" as part of this bibliographical appendix, I will list several prominent textbooks, treatises, and bibliographical resources that are available to readers who wish to learn more about the economic analysis of law.

There are now several textbooks and treatises that provide a good introduction to the field of law and economics generally. These include Robert Cooter & Thomas Ulen, Law and Economics (3rd ed. 2000), Richard A. Posner, Economic Analysis of Law (6th ed. 2003), and Steven Shavell, Foundations of Economic Analysis of Law (2003). At a more advanced level mathematically is Thomas J. Miceli, Economics of the Law: Torts, Contracts, Property, Litigation (1997). Another general book of note is David D. Friedman, Law's Order: What Economics Has to Do with Law and Why It Matters (2000).

Three more specialized books, all concerning accident law, should be mentioned because they were influential in the development of the field of law and economics. The earliest was the pathbreaking contribution by Guido Calabresi, The Costs of Accidents: A Legal and Economic Analysis (1970). This book was followed by more advanced treatments by William M. Landes & Richard A. Posner, The Economic Structure of Tort Law (1987) and Steven Shavell, Economic Analysis of Accident Law (1987).

Finally, there are three excellent bibliographic treatments of the field of law and economics. A comprehensive list of articles published through the early 1990s is available in Bibliography of Law and Economics (Boudewijn Bouckaert & Gerrit de Geest eds. 1992). Two more recent contributions, which include introductory essays on many specialized topics in law and economics, are The New Palgrave Dictionary of Economics and the Law, Vols. 1-3 (Peter Newman ed. 1998), and Encyclopedia of Law and Economics, Vols. I-V (Boudewijn Bouckaert & Gerrit de Geest eds. 2000).

Postscript: I still have been unable to find a source for the story of the beans and the can opener used in the introductory chapter of the book. As far as I know, it exists solely as part of the oral tradition of the economics profession.

INDEX

Absolute entitlement. *See* Entitlement, in nuisance law
Absolute liability. *See* Strict liability
Accident costs, noneconomic, 10 & n., 44n., 165-166. *See also* Nonstandardized goods, valuation of
Activity level
  drivers in automobile accidents, 50-54
  generally, 159-160
  pedestrians, in automobile accidents, 50-51, 54
  pollution victims, 112
Activity-level decision, 159-160
Administrative costs
  automobile accident law, 54-55
  insurance, 72-73
  taxes and transfers, 148 n.93, 153
Agent of a principal, 125
Assumptions, role of, 2-5
Automobile accident remedies
  contributory negligence defense, 49, 50, 54
  negligence, 45-46, 49-50, 52-54, 73, 75, 77, 151-152, 153, 161
  strict liability, 44-45, 48-49, 51-52, 53-54, 73-75, 76-77, 141-145, 151-153
Aversion to risk. *See* Risk aversion

Bargaining. *See* Coase Theorem; Cooperative behavior; Strategic behavior; Transaction costs
Bearing of risk. *See* Risk bearing
Beneficial risk, 59. *See also* Insurance; Risk bearing; Risk premium
Benefits, 10. *See also* Costs; Valuation of costs and benefits
Bias, in the valuation of costs and benefits. *See* Valuation of costs and benefits
Breach decision. *See* Efficient breach
Breach of contract remedies
  expectation damages, 30, 33-34, 35-36, 37-38, 39-40, 66, 150-151
  liquidated damages, 67-69
  reliance damages, 30, 34-35, 36, 38, 39-40, 66-67, 150-151
  restitution damages, 30, 35, 36, 38-40, 67, 150-151

Care. *See also* Care decision
  consumers in products liability situations, 120-121
  drivers in automobile accidents, 43-46, 71-72, 74
  generally, 159
  pedestrians in automobile accidents, 47-50
Care decision, 159
Coase Theorem, 13-16, 17, 29, 33, 43, 116n., 128n. *See also* Transaction costs
Co-insurance. *See* Insurance
Competitive markets, 103-106
Completely specified contract. *See* Contracts, fully specified
Conflict between efficiency and equity, 7-11, 147, 155-156, 162. *See also* Efficiency; Equity